REAGAN
A Political Biography

by

LEE EDWARDS

VIEWPOINT BOOKS
P.O. Box 9622
San Diego, California 92109

REAGAN
A Political Biography

© 1967 by Viewpoint Books

First Printing, October 1967

Printed in the United States of America

AUTHOR'S PREFACE

This is not an "authorized" biography or an "unauthorized" biography. It *is* a political biography based on nearly two years of research and writing; three lengthy visits to California; conversations with various members of the Reagan family, including the governor; bull sessions with Reagan aides and advisors; talks with political analysts and politicians of all persuasions in California, Washington, D. C., Chicago, New York and various points between; correspondence with Reagan friends, enemies, and acquaintances from coast to coast and overseas where actors and actresses sometimes settle; the compilation and study of thousands of newspaper and magazine clippings, speeches, statements, releases and other bits of Reaganalia.

I first met Ronald Reagan in October, 1965, when I was doing research for a possible *Reader's Digest* article about him. I was skeptical at first but by the end of my second day with him, I decided that here was no puppet at the end of a string but a highly intelligent, dedicated man with an intriguing personality and philosophy. The concept of this biography was born then.

Throughout 1966, my Reagan files grew and grew. In November, after his victory, I approached a publisher who quickly gave me the go-ahead. In February and again in June of 1967, I visited California, stopping in Sacramento, Los Angeles and

San Diego where I talked with anti- as well as pro-Reagan people. I noted a curious thing: no one, no matter how they disagreed with his politics, ever called Reagan a SOB. Knowing quite a few politicians, I was naturally impressed. And for the record let me add that Ronald Reagan will see his biography for the first time when everyone else does—when it's published.

This book would not have been possible without the research and editorial assistance of two people: Bruce Weinrod, who combed libraries and newspaper morgues for months, and Lo Anne Wagner, who has one of the fastest pencils and typewriters in town.

As always, I looked for encouragement and direction from my wife Anne, to whom this book is dedicated.

Lee Edwards
Washington, D. C.
August, 1967

CONTENTS

PROLOGUE   7
PART I: THE ACTOR   9
 1. A Little Country Town   11
 2. Down the Old Ox Road   18
 3. The Voice of the Chicago Cubs   26
 4. "Where's The Rest of Me?"   36
 5. Fort Roach   44
 6. Strikes, Communists and a Loaded Gun   51
 7. A Rendezvous with Destiny   65

PART II: THE CANDIDATE   81
 8. The *Only* Candidate   83
 9. Hat in the Ring   98
10. On the Hustings   108
11. The Creative Society   118
12. Landslide I   129
13. Common Sense and Nonsense   138
14. "A Prairie Fire"   151
15. Landslide II   171

PART III: THE GOVERNOR   181
16. "A Cause To Believe In"   183
17. Of, By and For the People   203

EPILOGUE   219
APPENDIX   235
INDEX   247

PROLOGUE

Time: Midnight, January 2, 1967.

Place: The brilliantly-illuminated, high-domed Rotunda of the State Capitol in Sacramento, Calif.

Cast: One hundred and fifty distinguished guests, including legislative leaders, friends and supporters, the seven-member gubernatorial party, one hundred and fifty representatives of the press, radio and television and assorted assistants.

Action: At one minute after midnight, the University of Southern California Chamber Singers, standing in an arc on the Rotunda balcony, sweetly sing "America, the Beautiful," *a capella*.

The Reverend Wilbur W. Y. Choy, his glasses glistening in the television lights, delivers the invocation.

United States Senator George Murphy, a former movie star and close friend of the governor-elect, administers the oath of office to 41-year-old Robert H. Finch, who had been elected lieutenant governor by the people of California less than two months before.

Climax: At sixteen minutes past midnight, the tall, handsome, youthful-looking man places his left hand on a 400-year-old Bible and, raising his right hand, is sworn in as the thirty-third governor of California by Justice Marshall F. McComb as they stand in front of a statue of Queen Isabella of Spain and Christopher Columbus.

There is an elongated second when time seems to stand still and then Governor Ronald Wilson Reagan steps in front of the microphones to break the tension in his own way:

"Well, George, here we are on the late show again...."

Laughter.

"I couldn't help that. I want you to know that this moment is not taken as lightly as such a remark might indicate."

After greeting those present, the justice, the new lieutenant governor, his old comrade Senator Murphy, and "those I love the most in all the world," he sums up his feelings simply and eloquently:

"Reverend, perhaps you weren't a part of my imagining of what this moment would be, but I am deeply grateful for your presence because you remind us, and bring here, the presence of someone else, without whose presence I certainly wouldn't have the nerve to do what I am going to try to do.

"Someone back in our history, I wasn't too good a student, but I think it was Benjamin Franklin who said, 'If ever someone could take public office and bring to public office the teachings and the precepts of the Prince of Peace, he would revolutionize the world and men would be remembering him for a thousand years.' I don't think anyone could ever take office and be so presumptuous to believe he could do that or that he could follow those precepts completely. I can tell you this, I'll try very hard. I think it is needed in today's world."

Amen.

PART ONE

THE ACTOR

Chapter One

A LITTLE COUNTRY TOWN

Tampico, Ill., is 86 miles from Chicago and 2006 miles from Sacramento, Calif. It's a cozy little town of barely 1000 inhabitants hiding in the heart of the fertile Midwest. It has a handsome park with a Civil War monument in its center, a railroad track on which trains used to chug and puff, and white clapboard houses with wide green lawns.

There on Feb. 6, 1911, Ronald Wilson Reagan was born. Ron was the younger of two boys, John Neil ("Moon") Reagan having been born over two years earlier, also in Tampico, on September 16, 1908. There were to be no other children. As the brand new baby cried out lustily, his father remarked: "For such a little bit of a fat Dutchman, he makes a hell of a lot of noise, doesn't he?"*

It was a typically boisterous remark by the new father, John Edward Reagan (pronounced Raygun). Jack Reagan was born in Bennett, Iowa, on July 13, 1883, and was orphaned at the age of three. He was reared by a succession of aunts and uncles, finally settling while still a youngster in Fulton, Ill. There he met pretty Nellie Clyde Wilson, a native of Fulton. Nellie was born on July 24, 1883. The two children grew up together in the

* "Dutch" still is Ronald Reagan's family nickname.

small Illinois town and were married there in 1906.

They made quite a contrast. Jack, standing almost six feet, was tall, muscular, of swarthy complexion with thick, wavy, brown hair. Nellie was small and slender with light brown hair and blue eyes. He was outspoken, quick-tempered, a natural raconteur. She was gentle and soft-spoken. He was Catholic, an indifferent churchgoer; she was Protestant and deeply religious. He was too fond of alcohol, she was a teetotaler.

The Reagans were Democrats. Jack was staunch in his views. Nellie, in her older son's words, "just went along." Ron and Neil followed their father and also counted themselves Democrats, although Neil became a Republican after voting for Franklin Delano Roosevelt in 1932.

A fierce individualist, Jack Reagan believed literally, according to his sons, that all men were created equal. Ron recalls that when the film, *The Birth of a Nation*, came to town, "my brother and I were the only kids not to see it." Explained their father, "It deals with the Ku Klux Klan against the colored folks, and I'm damned if anyone in this family will go see it."

Jack tried to enlist in the armed forces during World War I, but was rejected because he was married and had two children.

He was never a financial success. He never owned his own home and he never made more than $55 a week at any time in his life. Comments his younger son: "Our family didn't exactly come from the wrong side of the tracks, but we were certainly always within sound of the train whistles." Both sons went to work when barely in their teens.

Jack Reagan was "in" shoes, working variously

as a shoe clerk, the manager of a shoe department and part-owner of a shoe store. His younger son remembers that he "loved shoes" and "even studied a correspondence course about how to sell more sabots, and spent hours analyzing the bones of the foot." But Jack loved the bottle too, like many an Irishman before him, and this weakness coupled with frequent bad investments kept him an also-ran in business—although he was always welcome wherever he went because of his rib-tickling, story-telling ability. Jack never completed grade school. Nellie did but went no further. However, both were avid readers and their home was always filled with books. Mrs. Reagan, in fact, arranged regular readings of plays and stories for the various ladies societies in Tampico and the other Illinois towns in which the Reagans lived. Nellie and Jack frequently played the leads.

By the time Ron was nine, he had lived in a number of small Illinois towns west of Chicago as well as the Windy City itself for a brief period: Tampico, Galesburg, Monmouth, Tampico again, and at last Dixon, where the Reagans put down roots until Ron was past twenty-one. Frequently, Neil Reagan recalls, "The Reagan family really didn't know where the next buck was coming from, but Nellie always had the right outlook on life and was sure that, 'Before the next payment was due, God would find a way.'"

In a letter to this writer, Neil Reagan described the Dixon, Ill., of 1920:

"At that time Dixon was a town of about 10,000, built on gently rolling northern Illinois hills. The Rock River cut through the heart of town with one bridge across the river in those days. There was a large Borden Milk plant, a wire screen factory, a

J. I. Case Plow Company factory and a Portland Cement plant in the town. It was a bustling town, progressive, and the county seat of Lee County.

"The courthouse stood in the middle of a square across the street from the Nachusa Tavern, which still stands and is still operated as a hotel. Its claim to fame, as well as being a fine hotel, is that on occasion Abraham Lincoln, General Grant and celebrities of that era enjoyed its hospitality. We, as youngsters, always held it sort of in awe."

There was also the Family Theatre, a public library and Dixon High School, for which Ron passionately desired to play football. The game attracted him because of its physical challenge and because his extremely poor eyesight would not be a handicap. Baseball was impossible—he couldn't see a pitch until it was practically at the end of his bat. Contact lenses, which Reagan wears today, were not available in those days but in football, in the line, you only had to see a few feet in all directions.

When Dutch entered Dixon High School he was only 5'3" and weighed 108 pounds, a size more suitable for manager than player. But he persisted and in the middle of his junior year he became and stayed a regular at right guard. He also read just about everything he could find in the library, including Horatio Alger. He had the lead in several high school plays and in the opinion of an unbiased observer, his brother, "was very good." Ron capped his high school career by being elected president of the student body in his senior year.

Comments a fellow student, football player and actor, R. A. McNichol: "Dutch was a very capable, loyal and personable individual with strong convictions—and a determination to accomplish that in which he believes."

According to Bernard J. Frazer, who taught social science at Dixon High School and had many talks with young Reagan: "He happens to be an example of that rare individual who carried into adulthood most of the dreams and enthusiasm for life that he had in youth. Perhaps he was more idealistic; perhaps more fortunate in his experiences and the influences which shaped them, than most youngsters. For example, his very unusual mother had that rare ability to make the ideal and fine seem quite practical to others."

Frazer remembers that his young pupil "was a natural leader in school activities . . . endowed with a curious, keen and retentive mind."

He was an instinctive crusader. "In high school," says the former teacher, "he, as do many young people, bled for humanity and deplored the world's materialism, its selfishness and inability to cooperate. However, even then he seemed to feel that, if they so desired, men could shape their own destiny. To him, as a teenager, the idea of the State taking over, or even attempting to control the individual's choices was very distasteful."

In the summers Dutch worked. When he was fourteen he was a construction worker at 35¢ an hour on a ten-hour day, six-day week. His specialty: digging foundations in heavy clay and soil. In the summer of 1925 he made $200 but did not spend it. In his own words, "I knew it was for something else—college."

The next summer, at 15, he got a job he was to keep for seven summers—lifeguard at Lowell Park, a recreation area on the Rock River. His salary was $15 a week. During his stay at Lowell Park (named after the poet, James Russell Lowell), Reagan estimates that he saved 77 people. "The only money I ever got," he recalls, "was ten dollars for diving for an old man's upper plate that he lost going down our slide."

Ron was saving for one particular school: Eureka College, located some 70 miles south of Dixon and 20 miles from Peoria, Ill. College was *not* the normal next step for a high school graduate in the late 1920's. In fact, less than 10 percent of the graduating seniors then went on to a college or university. (The figure in 1966 was 55 percent.) Furthermore, the economy was beginning to show the stresses and strains which were to erupt so tragically on Black Tuesday, Oct. 29, 1929.

Although it had a modest tuition and other expenses, Eureka still cost $900 a year—a considerable sum for a family like the Reagans with their uneven income. Also, in those days, there was widespread feeling that college demanded four years that would be better occupied earning a living.

One Reagan brother agreed—at least for a while. "My brother Neil," remembers Ronald Reagan, "thought college was a waste of time; also an impossibility, if you had to do it on your own."

Not so Ron, who selected Eureka College for a number of reasons: (1) it was small, less than 250 students; (2) it was co-educational, about half boys and half girls; (3) it had a good football team; (4) it was run by the Christian Church, of which Ronald Reagan is a member today; and, (5) the most important factor of all for the 17-year-old young man, his high school sweetheart, Margaret Cleaver, had announced her intention to attend Eureka.

A LITTLE COUNTRY TOWN

However, despite the summer savings he had so carefully accumulated, Ron still did not have enough money for the $180 tuition, plus room and board. Using his ability to persuade others, that would later impress political observers, the young student argued his case. Eureka officials considered the applicant's athletic ability, the earnings from his summer jobs, his obvious eagerness to attend their school. They offered him a scholarship for half his tuition and a job for his board. He would have to pay for his room and any luxuries out of his savings. It wasn't any free ride, but it was all the aid Ron needed.

In the fall of 1928, he entered Eureka College with pride to equal any freshman Ivy Leaguer—and determination to meet the challenge and justify the faith of the school dons.

Chapter Two

DOWN THE OLD OX ROAD

During his four years at Eureka, Ron Reagan played a lot of football, joined a fraternity, fell in and out of love, read several hundred books, won an acting award in a national play contest, was elected student body president and participated in his first strike. Through it all, money continued to be so serious a problem that he almost didn't return to school after his freshman year.

The young student was now 6'1" tall and weighed 175 pounds. He had thick brown hair, blue eyes and a ready smile. He quickly pledged Tau Kappa Epsilon, one of the more prestigious national fraternities on campus. He became a reporter for the school paper, *The Pegasus*. Within a few weeks of arrival, he was tabbed as a sure Big Man on Campus. It was almost natural, therefore, that he should be picked as the freshman representative on the strike committee.

The campus strike followed in the wake of a decision by Eureka President Burt Wilson to cut the curriculum. The cut was part of a proposed economy program designed to save Eureka, whose normal sources of financial support were being dried up by the impending Depression. The plan, in Reagan's words, called for such drastic academic reductions "that many juniors and seniors would have been cut off without the courses needed for graduation in their chosen majors. Needless to say, the faculty would have been decimated and Eureka would have lost its high academic standing."

The student body, with the approval of "almost every professor on campus," submitted a counterplan to the president who rejected it. The students then presented a petition, signed by 143 of the 220 students, including Reagan, to the college's board of trustees demanding the resignation of President Wilson. Meeting this challenge head on, Wilson announced that he had submitted his own resignation. Friendly faculty members and other sources, however, revealed that the trustees intended to reject the resignation, give Wilson a vote of confidence and discipline the student body.

The Eureka students also made plans. It was near midnight the following week, Nov. 27, 1928, when the trustees emerged from their conference with the president. To their great surprise, they were greeted by a student committee, including freshman Ron Reagan, who wanted to know their decision. Informed that the trustees had indeed rejected Wilson's resignation, the students gave a pre-arranged signal. The "old college bell started tolling," calling the student body and faculty to the chapel. There, freshman Ron Reagan delivered a ringing, dramatic speech.

"When I came to actually presenting the motion," Reagan remembers, "there was no need for parliamentary procedure; they came to their feet with a roar—even the faculty members present voted by acclamation. It was heady wine."

After Thanksgiving, the students put their simple plan into effect: no attendance at classes until their demands were met. Few attended any classes. (Two students who did were President Wilson's two daughters.) Professors went to their classrooms and marked all absentees present. To pass the time, the strike committee sponsored a dance every afternoon but always ended it at four o'clock—for basketball practice.

Studies, however, were not neglected. The strike committee established study hours and enforced them; it even made up assignments which were scrupulously carried out. In Reagan's words, "ours was no riotous burning in effigy but a serious, well-planned program, engineered from the ground up by students but with the full support and approval of almost every professor on the campus."

News of the strike spread quickly. Reporters converged on Eureka and the strike committee set up a "regular press headquarters" to service the gentlemen of the Fourth Estate. To counteract the administration, which was flooding the campus with mimeographed statements, a faculty-student panel was formed to issue regular bulletins.

After one week of suffering these slings and arrows, President Wilson again offered his resignation. The trustees, by a 7-5 vote, accepted it. Meetings were held between the trustees, students and faculty. An amicable understanding was arrived at. The strike was called off, the faculty agreed to withhold any salary demands for "an indefinite period," and Eureka returned to normalcy.

Despite the excitement and rewards of his first year, Ron Reagan returned home that summer wondering whether Eureka was for him. By fall, he had decided not to return to college but to take a job as a surveyor's assistant. He had decided he couldn't afford Eureka even with the scholarship and the job. More importantly in the mind of the young athlete, he believed the football coach, Ralph McKinzie, was "against" him and would *never* let him play. Ron bid a sorrowful farewell to his sweetheart, Margaret, who was returning to Eureka. But with the dawn came a torrent of rain and no surveying for the day. The young man rode back to Eureka with his girl for a visit, saw the football coach and the inviting new football uniforms, found a job washing dishes in the girls' dormitory, was told by the college that it would defer half of tuition until after graduation and decided to stay at Eureka after all.

In his autobiography, *Where's the Rest of Me?*,* published in 1965, Reagan waxes lyrical about the next three years:

"Oh, it was a small town, a small school, with small doings. It was in a poor time without money, without ceremony, with pleasant thoughts of the past to balance fears of the uncertain future . . . . Those were the nights when we spent all of twenty cents on a date: two big cherry phosphates at the drug counter (with the big colored jars of water lighted up) and a walk home. Or when we danced in somebody's house or in the fraternity living rooms under the dimmest of lights, while the chaperones—always old Eureka grads who had met each other this way themselves—took a turn around outside or just dozed. Or when we devoured homemade cake and repressed heartburnings of a different sort as we strolled under the campus elms. And there was the wonderful thing of inviting older people who knew some jokes and the ways of the world and how to talk to us with-

---

* *Where's the Rest of Me?* by Ronald Reagan with Richard G. Hubler, Duell, Sloan & Pearce.

out condescending; scrambling eggs before an open fire and talking about Hoover and his calm statements on prosperity; whipping up the hot chocolate and shaking our heads over this upstart Franklin D. Roosevelt, who was beginning to criticize from New York."

Through with sulking, Ron decided he was going to show Coach McKinzie how wrong he had been about his playing. By the third Saturday he was starting at right guard and for three seasons "averaged all but two minutes of every game." In the spring, he went out for the swimming team and eventually wound up as captain. He also tried out for track and won his letter in that sport as well.

It was easy to keep in training because Eureka took its religion seriously. Bible courses were required and daily chapel was mandatory during the week. Smoking was not allowed on campus and in Neil Reagan's words, "the thought of having a drink was unheard of." The training took: Ronald Reagan never has smoked and takes only an occasional drink.

In between sports and classes, Ron joined the campus dramatic society and enrolled in the dramatics course under Miss Ellen Marie Johnson, who saw talent in the tall, handsome young man with the resonant, baritone voice. The high point of his collegiate dramatic career came in his junior year when Miss Johnson entered Eureka in the annual one-act play contest sponsored by Northwestern University. Only 12 colleges and universities were invited to present their plays out of hundreds of applicants from across the country. Eureka, which had chosen Edna St. Vincent Millay's fantasy, *Aria da Capo,* was one of the twelve and the *only* school without a drama department to be so honored.

Writes Reagan: "Ours was really a homegrown effort, with Grecian costumes copied from our history books and sewed together by coeds in the various sororities. Quarterback Bud Cole and I played the Greek shepherd boys who carry the anti-war plot. My high spot was a death scene wherein I was strangled by Bud. No actor can ask for more. Dying is the way to live in the theater."

To almost everyone's amazement, especially the actors in *Aria da Capo*, Eureka finished second, and Ron Reagan was one of six actors who received awards for their dramatic excellence. After the contest, the head of Northwestern's drama department asked Ron if he had ever considered the stage as a career. Some fertile seeds had been planted.

There was politics too. Ron was elected president of his fraternity, Tau Kappa Epsilon. For three years, he served as president of the Booster Club, the student organization which coordinated the annual homecoming weekend with its football game, alumni banquet, dance and other entertainments. He was also the principal basketball cheer leader, three years the school's top swimmer, one year its swimming coach and two years the feature editor of the year book. Finally, as a rising senior he was elected president of Eureka's student body.

Football coach McKinzie has said: "Dutch was not an outstanding football player, but he was a good plugger, dedicated, put out a lot, had a lot of spirit and desire. He got some scholarship help, but mostly worked his way through school by waiting on tables, washing windows and raking lawns. He was ambitious and determined. Nobody was paying the bills for him."

Ernest E. Higdon, who taught Reagan at Eureka, has said: "He's one of the finest men I've ever known. I don't agree with his politics; I'm a Democrat. But if I had lived in California I'd have voted for him, because I know him and what he stands for."

More gratifying than all these honors, perhaps, was the decision by his brother Neil to enroll at Eureka. In the Reagan tradition, Neil got a job working in the coeds' kitchen and a scholarship to play football. Ron did not discover until years later why his brother decided to quit the cement plant in Dixon and go to school:

"Working in a grimy atmosphere of limestone dust, Moon (a nickname since high school) was teamed with an elderly immigrant who could barely manage our language. This oddly assorted pair became friends and exchanged information as men will about their families and backgrounds. The old man constantly queried Moon as to why he wasn't in college as I was. Then one day very quietly he presented Moon with the alternative to college. 'Look at me—we'll alvays vork together, chust you and me, and someday you'll be chust like me—isn't that nize?' (The old man) never mentioned it again—he didn't have to."

One sun-bright June day in 1932, Ronald Wilson Reagan was graduated from Eureka College with a degree in economics and sociology. He had earned his letter in football, track and swimming. He had served as student body president. He had played the lead in several dramatic plays and had won an acting award in a national competition. The campus was agreed that Ron Reagan was bound to succeed—but where? He was 21 years old and broke. An old friend of the family asked him: "What do you think you'd like to do?"

Ron had a ready answer: "Show business."

Chapter Three

THE VOICE OF THE CHICAGO CUBS

"The problem," recalls Reagan, "was how to go about it. Broadway and Hollywood were as inaccessible as outer space." He decided to try his luck closer to home in a phase of show business where his fine voice would be an asset—radio. Specifically, he aspired to be a sports announcer.

Neil Reagan remembers well his brother's determination to succeed: "While still in college he decided that he would be a sports announcer on radio, drove us nuts in the fraternity as he walked around broadcasting imaginary football games play by play and never lost sight of this goal until he landed the job at WOC in Davenport, Iowa."

At the end of summer, Ron hitchhiked to Chicago, the center of American radio in the Thirties. He had no contacts, no letters of introduction, and no experience. For several days, he walked the hard pavements of Chicago, visiting the outlets of the major networks as well as large and small independent stations, like WGN. He got nowhere, except at NBC he was told that the program director interviews "on Thursdays." On Thursday, Ron timidly explained to the girl at the reception desk why he was there. A lady appeared from the inner sanctum and, seated on a couch in the reception room, listened to the young man's story.

Her reaction and advice were to the point: You have no experience. This is the "big time." Try to get a job with one of the smaller stations "in the sticks" and then come back and see me.

As so often in his life, Ron took the good advice and hitchhiked 100 miles back to Dixon, unfortunately traveling the last 30 miles with a man who had been hunting skunks. That night over supper, Jack Reagan listened to his son's experiences and then offered him the family Oldsmobile to visit radio stations in the general neighborhood.

The following Monday, Ron made his first call at Station WOC, located in Davenport, Iowa, 75 miles away. He asked to see the program director, who turned out to be a veteran of vaudeville, born in Scotland, named Peter MacArthur.

"Where the hell have ye been?" MacArthur roared in his Highland burr. "Don't ye ever listen to the radio?"

It seemed that for one month WOC had been advertising for a staff announcer and had hired one out of 95 applicants only the week before.

Young Reagan's temper flared and he abruptly left, crying out behind him: "How in hell does a guy ever get to be a sports announcer if he can't get inside a station?"

Reagan was standing at the elevator when he heard a great thumping and loud talking down the hallway. A cane rapped him on the shin. It was MacArthur, who, crippled by arthritis, used two canes to move about.

"Do ye perhaps know football?" asked the program director, scowling.

The would-be announcer replied that he had

played the game for eight years and before he could say anything else, he was led into a vacant studio and told to describe a football game "and make me see it."

More than a little bewildered, Reagan looked at the heavy blue velvet covering the walls and then at the microphone. The red lights flashed "On" and Ron began describing, from memory, the fourth quarter of a game played between Western State University and Eureka College the previous fall. Twenty minutes later, wringing wet from tension and determination, he wound up his "broadcast" with the traditional, "we return you now to our main studio."

MacArthur entered the studio, chuckling and growling at the same time. "You did great! Now, luke, we have a sponsor for four University of Iowa games. Ye be here a week from Saturday and I'll give ye five dollars and bus fare. If ye do all right on that one, ye'll do the other three."

Ronald Reagan had convinced a 30-year veteran in the business that he could handle the job—no mean feat for a 21-year old who had never stood before a microphone before.

The following Saturday after the University of Iowa game, MacArthur told the rookie announcer without any hyperbole, "Ye'll do the rest of the games." He was even given a raise: $10 a game plus bus fare.

At the end of the season, Ron returned to Dixon to wait for the call he fervently hoped would come. Finally, it did, a few days after New Year's Day, 1933. An announcer had left WOC and MacArthur offered Ron one hundred dollars a month as a staff announcer.

"My bag," Reagan says, "and you can keep that

THE VOICE OF THE CHICAGO CUBS

singular—was packed, and I moved to Davenport. I was hired, I would be fired, I would be rehired, but I was out in the world at last."

At home, Jack Reagan went to work for the Federal government (Franklin Delano Roosevelt had been elected and as a long-loyal Democrat, Jack was rewarded). The senior Reagan distributed foodstuffs as well as government scrip which the poor and needy used at the grocery. Dixon was hard hit: the cement plant for which "Moon" had worked closed down, adding one thousand more to the already long list of unemployed.

Jack spent much of his time finding and assigning jobs for the unemployed. He worked days and nights on a schedule of rotating jobs so that every man would have at least a couple of days work at a stretch.

But then welfare workers arrived from back East with files and furniture to begin institutionalizing the process. "Wheels," remarks Ronald Reagan, "were turning in Washington and government was busy at the job it does best—growing." The day inevitably came when Jack offered a week's work to a group of men, who replied, "Jack, we can't take it." They explained that the last time they took jobs the welfare office had cut off their relief. When they stopped working, several days later, they had to reopen their "case" at the welfare office and submit to new interviews, applications and cards. "The process took three weeks," recalls Reagan, "and in the meantime their families went hungry—all because they'd done a few days' honest work."

Shortly thereafter, Jack Reagan was appointed local administrator of the Works Progress Administration (WPA). Under his direction, there were no boondoggles in Dixon and he constantly came up with ingenious projects for the able-bodied men of Dixon. Once he even figured out a way to use the old streetcar rails, torn from the main street, as structural steel in a hanger at the new airport.

And all the while he battled the "welfare band" who used every pretext, including physical unfitness, to resist "releasing their charges to WPA."

It was Ronald Reagan's first close look at the ways of the Federal government and it made a lasting impression.

At Station WOC, Ron was having problems. To this day, he is not good at reading a manuscript.* He tried to read the commercials they gave him, but without much success. His voice was stiff and wooden. He knew it and so did the sponsors. Before long he was told he would be replaced as a staff announcer but would be "kept in mind" for sports events.

His replacement arrived and Ron was directed to break him in. But when the new man learned the circumstances of his predecessor's dismissal, he demanded a contract. WOC's management refused and Ron was asked to stay on "for the time being." Reagan vowed to show the station he could be an announcer, commercials and all. The challenge was just what he needed. With his adrenalin flowing freely, he read every piece of copy they handed him like an old pro and very soon there was no more talk of a replacement.

Reagan rose swiftly to the top of his profession, becoming one of the best known sports announcers

* As governor, he rarely uses a prepared text, preferring to speak from 3 x 5 index cards which he has personally researched and written.

in the Midwest. His rise was boosted considerably when WOC merged with its sister station, WHO, to become WHO Des Moines, NBC's key station in the Corn Belt. WHO built a 50 kilowatt transmitter, one of only 12 such rigs in the country. Ron's salary went to $75 a week—plus bonuses and fees for "touring the banquet circuit, writing a guest column, and hiring out to handle public-address system chores at events we weren't broadcasting."

One of the other announcers at WHO was Ed Reimers, the now famous man with the cupped hands for Allstate Insurance ("You're in safe hands at Allstate."). Reimers describes Reagan as "a great sports announcer . . . a good actor . . . certainly one of the better presidents the Screen Actors Guild has ever had . . . If he's half as good a governor as he was a sportscaster he'll be great . . . . I'm proud to know him. I'd be proud to know him even if he wasn't governor."

Congressman H. R. Gross of Iowa, who has become nationally famous for his careful scrutiny of the fine print in the Federal budget, was also on WHO's staff in the 1930's as a newscaster. He remembers "Dutch" as an "outstanding sports announcer—he was actually sports editor of the station—and very popular in the state of Iowa. I always thought he had very strong political possibilities. . . . He was conscientious, he had ability, he was honest and decent. What else can you say about a man?"

Reagan estimates that during this period he broadcast 45 college football games from every "major press box in the Midwest," covered more than 600 major league baseball games by telegraph, and handled swimming meets and track meets as well. He interviewed famous sports personalities, including Doc Kearns, former manager of Jack Dempsey, Ed "Strangler" Lewis, and Max Baer. He also remembers meeting the English actor and Hollywood star, Leslie Howard, at a fundraising event for victims of an Ohio River flood.

One night he even interviewed the famous evangelist, Aimee Semple McPherson. Unfamiliar with her work, Ron let Mrs. McPherson do most of the talking which she did beautifully until she suddenly said "good night," with four minutes to go on the program. Not knowing enough about the evangelist to fill the remaining time himself, Ron made a circular motion with his hand, the signal for the playing of a phonograph record.

"A sleepy engineer in the control room," he recounts, "reached out, pulled a record off a stack, put it on the turntable, and nodded to go ahead. In my most dulcet tones, I said, 'Ladies and gentlemen, we conclude this broadcast by the noted evangelist, Aimee Semple McPherson, with a brief interlude of transcribed music.' I expected nothing less than the 'Ave Maria.' The Mills Brothers started singing 'Minnie the Moocher's Wedding Day.'"

One Friday night, Reagan invented a new program which became "a steppingstone for someone else's career." Given a half hour to play records, Reagan presented nothing but college songs and filled in the gaps with the next day's schedule of football games plus predictions of the winners. On a subsequent Friday night, his brother, Neil, who had graduated from Eureka, was seated in the studio. Neil began shaking his head in disagreement about some of his brother's predictions. Ron switched on the mike and the two brothers de-

THE VOICE OF THE CHICAGO CUBS

bated back and forth for a half hour about the games, promising the audience at the conclusion that they would report who had the best percentage the following Friday.

The joint appearance led, Reagan tells, "to a fifteen-dollar-a-week job for Moon, doing the football scoreboard on Saturday nights because I was still out of town on my football broadcasts. That job led Moon to an announcing job at the reinstituted WOC in Davenport, to program directing, network producing, and his present position in Los Angeles as vice president of an advertising agency."*

While in Des Moines, Ron fulfilled one of his basic loves—riding—by applying for a commission in the U.S. Cavalry Reserves. The opportunity to ride wonderful mounts and receive expert training in horsemanship was irresistible to Reagan, who says, "I think the Irish are one of the lost tribes of the Arabs." He avoided a physical examination for years because of his poor eyesight and then bluffed his way through the exam to become a second lieutenant on June 18, 1937.**

During one bitter cold Iowa winter, Reagan decided that he would be a much better voice of the Chicago Cubs if he accompanied the team on its spring training trip to Catalina Island, only 50 miles across the water from warm, sun-drenched Los Angeles. He told the station that the trip would provide him with "color and atmosphere" for the coming season. To his delight, they agreed

---

* Neil Reagan is national vice president in charge of radio and television programming for the giant agency, McCann-Erickson.

** Reagan wore glasses most of the time then, uses contact lenses today and Benjamin Franklin half-glasses over them for very heavy reading.

and he took his first trip west of Kansas City.

He made the annual trip to Catalina Island until the spring of 1937 when a growing restlessness and dissatisfaction gripped him. Sports announcing had become too confining. One night, while in Los Angeles, he visited an alumna of WHO, Joy Hodges, who was singing at the Biltmore Bowl. Over dinner, Reagan told Joy about the Des Moines theater manager who had suggested a screen test for him, the performers on the WHO program who had been hired for a Hollywood film, and the fact that he had picked sports announcing five years before as a path to acting. What did *she* think?

"Take off your glasses," was her first remark. Then she set up an appointment with a Hollywood agent, William Meiklejohn, who "will be honest with you." But, "for heaven's sake," she persisted, "don't see him with those glasses on!"

Reagan remembers this as a very funny line for "without the glasses I couldn't see him at all—but the important thing was, he'd see me."

The next morning Meiklejohn listened to Reagan outline his acting experience, his salary needs and his high hopes. The young announcer concluded: "Should I go back to Des Moines and forget this, or what do I do?"

The agent picked up the telephone, dialed Warner Brothers and asked for Max Arnow, the casting director. "Max," said Meiklejohn without any preliminaries, "I have another Robert Taylor in my office."

Arnow's booming reply was quite audible: "God made only one Robert Taylor!"

Nevertheless Arnow invited them over and after sizing up Reagan's shoulders and listening to his

THE VOICE OF THE CHICAGO CUBS

voice, scheduled a screen test the following Tuesday—a scene from Philip Barry's play, *Holiday*.

Reagan did the scene, after the make-up man had tried vainly to do something with his crew-cut. When it was over, he was informed that it would be several days before Jack Warner could see the film and of course he would stand by. To which the young Midwesterner replied, "No, I will be on the train tomorrow—me and the Cubs are going home."

On the train, he wondered whether he "had blown the whole thing" but reflected that at least he had a good story to tell. As Reagan has since written, "I had done, through ignorance, the smartest thing it was possible to do. Hollywood just *loves* people who don't need Hollywood."

Before he was back in Des Moines one day, a telegram arrived: "Warners offer contract seven years, one year's option, starting at $200 a week. What shall I do? Meiklejohn."

Reagan sent an immediate reply: "Sign before they change their minds." And then he yelled a yell of joy and delight as only a small town boy from Illinois can who is going to Hollywood to be a movie star. He was 26.

Chapter Four

"WHERE'S THE REST OF ME?"

Warner Brothers liked Ronald Reagan very much. During his first 11 months, he appeared in eight pictures—an unusually heavy schedule for an unknown actor who had never appeared on Broadway or been inside a film studio. Most young contract players wait months before getting a part. But not Reagan, who was immediately given the lead in a 61-minute film called *Love Is On the Air*. It was a "B" picture, as were most of the pictures in which he would appear for several years. The young actor didn't mind: "All I knew was I was starring in my first movie, and that seemed to make a great deal of sense."

During that first year, he learned how to keep his head still in close-ups; to watch for the chalk marks on the floor which marked your position for that scene; to review in the evening the "rushes" of that day's filming; and how to make love, which was just about the most difficult challenge of all.

"I discovered," he remembers, "that a kiss is only beautiful to the two people engaged in doing it. If you really kiss the girl, it shoves her face out of shape . . . . This was not my only fault. My head was casting a shadow by getting in the path of her key light; my collar was pulled out of shape by the position of my arm; all in all, I had to draw back and start over with the realization that work is work, fun is fun, and kissing was more fun at the high school picnic."

He also lost forever, at least publicly, the nickname of Dutch, an appellation which caused unrestrained shudders in Warner's publicity department.

Picture followed on picture: *Submarine D-1* and *Hollywood Hotel* (in 1937); *Swing Your Lady, Sergeant Murphy, Accidents Will Happen, Girls on Probation, Boy Meets Girl, Cowboy From Brooklyn, Brother Rat* and *Going Places* (in 1938), and many others. In his own words, Ronald Reagan became "the Errol Flynn of the B's. I was as brave as Errol, but in a low-budget fashion." The films usually took three weeks to make. They were rewrites and remakes of movies which were good enough for one more variation on an old familiar theme. Today, such "B" films make up much of television's nightly fare. Like Flynn, Reagan did many of his own stunts—fighting, jumping, diving and the like. He was encouraged to do so: it enabled the director to cut his schedule in half by shooting over the villain's shoulder on Ron's face for most of the fight.

Reagan made friends quickly and easily: established stars like Pat O'Brien, Dick Powell, Jimmy Cagney, Humphrey Bogart, Frank McHugh and others took to the keen-witted young man who worked so hard at his trade.

He was given a good part in what turned out to be a highly successful film and a solid money maker: *Brother Rat*, the story of three cadets at Virginia Military Institute. The other stars were Eddie Albert, who had the lead in the Broadway version, Wayne Morris and Jane Wyman, who became Reagan's romantic interest off camera and ultimately his wife in 1940. They were married in Wee Kirk O'Heather Chapel in Glendale, Calif., on January 26. A daughter, Maureen Elizabeth, was born in 1941. In 1945, they adopted a boy, Michael. They were divorced on June 28, 1948, after eight years of marriage.

Miss Wyman had been married once before to manufacturer Myron Futterman, and was divorced from Futterman in December, 1938. Reagan has never talked publicly about his divorce from Jane Wyman. During the divorce proceedings in 1948, Miss Wyman stated that she did not share her husband's intense interest in politics and the Screen Actors Guild. In answer to a question put by Judge Thurmond Clarke, she explained she had nothing against the Guild but that "most of their discussions were far above me."

In his autobiography, Reagan wrote: "The problem hurt our children most . . . There is no easy way to break up a home, and I don't think there is any way to ease the bewildered pain of children at such times." Maureen is now Mrs. David Sills and lives in Anaheim, Calif., with her young lawyer husband. She is very active in Republican politics and campaigned for her father on the platform and over radio and television in the 1966 gubernatorial election. Michael Reagan is a dispatcher for a Los Angeles trucking firm.

With the release of *Brother Rat,* Ronald Reagan was assured of steady employment if not yet stardom, and brought his mother and father to Hollywood. Although Jack Reagan's heart condition severely limited what he could do, his actor son put him in charge of handling his fan mail.

"WHERE'S THE REST OF ME?"

The responsibility satisfied his father's desire to feel useful and the son's concern lest the job be too taxing. Until his death in 1941, Jack Reagan continued to help his son.

Everybody has a special picture which he thinks should be made. For Ronald Reagan, it was the story of Knute Rockne, the legendary football coach at Notre Dame. As he explains, "I had no intention of playing Rockne. I had always seen Pat O'Brien as the logical star in the title role. I had something else in mind for myself—a fellow named George Gipp."

Reagan lobbied all over Hollywood, asking everyone how you went about transforming an idea into a picture. One day he picked up a copy of *Variety*, the motion picture trade paper, to read that Warner Brothers was going to do the life story of Knute Rockne, with Pat O'Brien in the starring role!

He immediately called on a director and good friend, Brynie Foy, who told him, grinning all the while, "You talk too much." Reagan quickly explained that all he was interested in was the part of George Gipp. Foy replied: "Well, you'd better do something because they've already tested ten fellows for the part." Ron made an appointment to see Robert Fellows, the film's producer.

But Fellows declined to believe that Ronald Reagan could play the part and kept repeating over and over again: "Gipp was the greatest player in the country." Protests by the broad-shouldered actor that he had played football for eight years and had even won a football scholarship to college had no effect.

Then, Reagan remembered the advice of a friend: "You have to realize these fellows only believe what they see on film." He abruptly left the producer's office for his home where he uncovered several photographs from his football days at Eureka College. Within minutes he was back at the studio, and invading the producer's sanctum once again, "slapped the pictures down on his desk . . . I was smart enough to keep my mouth shut and let the photographs talk."

Fellows asked if he could keep the photographs. Reagan replied simply, "Sure," and drove home slowly. He had been in his house barely fifteen minutes when the telephone rang. He was to test for the part of George Gipp at eight o'clock the next morning.

He got the part, which although it occupied only one reel of the picture, was "a nearly perfect part from an actor's standpoint. A great entrance, an action middle, and a death scene to finish up." *Knute Rockne, All American* was sneak-previewed in Pasadena in the early fall of 1940. The next morning, before he was even out of bed, Warner Brothers telephoned Reagan to tell him he had been cast as the second lead in an Errol Flynn picture, *Santa Fe Trail*. "A new door had been opened," he recalls. "Suddenly there were people on the lot greeting me who hadn't previously acknowledged my existence."

That morning at the studio Reagan watched a wardrobe man rush into the fitting room. "Without a word, he gathered the completed uniforms (of the actor who had initially been cast) in one arm, threw them in a corner, and hung the new ones in their place. It occurred to me then that it would be just as easy someday to throw my clothes in the corner and hang some other actor's in their place."

But such black possibilities were then exceedingly unlikely in the mind of Ronald Reagan.

The parts and the pictures got better and better: *The Badman,* with Wallace Beery and Lionel Barrymore; *International Squadron,* in which he played the lead, and finally in 1941, *King's Row,* which made Ronald Reagan a Hollywood star, and, paradoxically, made him begin to wonder whether that was all he wanted to be.

Reagan played the part of Drake McHugh, a happy-go-lucky ladies' man in a small town who had spent most of a rather large inheritance. His key scene came when he awakened in his own bed to realize that his two legs had been amputated following an accident in a railroad yard. His line was: "Where's the rest of me?"

He has written: "A whole actor would find such a scene difficult; giving it the necessary dramatic impact as half an actor was murderous. I felt I had neither the experience nor the talent to fake it. I simply had to find out how it really felt, short of actual amputation."

He rehearsed the scene for days. He delivered the line a hundred different ways. He talked to disabled people "trying to brew in myself the caldron of emotions a man must feel who wakes up one sunny morning to find half of himself gone." Despite all his rehearsal and research, he still felt he had not penetrated the heart of the scene.

The morning of the shooting, uncertain of how to read the line, Reagan walked over to the set in his nightshirt. There he found that the prop men had cut a hole in the mattress of the bed and put a supporting box underneath. On an overwhelming impulse, he climbed into the rig and spent almost an hour there, staring at the smooth bottom of the bed where his legs should have been.

"Gradually," he remembers, "the affair began to terrify me. In some weird way, I felt something terrible had happened to my body." The director, Sam Wood, quietly gave the word, "Action!" and there was the sharp *clack* of the wooden clapper board which signals the beginning of every scene. Reagan looked down at the flat surface of the bed, tried to reach for his legs and then called out the question which had been haunting him for weeks: "Where's the rest of me?"

The question continued to haunt Ronald Reagan for 25 years—until he finally and ultimately answered it in 1966 when he ran for the office of governor of California.

In his autobiography, written in 1963 many months before he decided to run for public office, and while he still thought of himself as an actor, Reagan revealed why he finally found himself in politics:

"If he is only an actor, I feel, he is much like I was in *King's Row*, only half a man—no matter how great his talents. I regard acting with the greatest affection; it has made my life for me. But I realize it tends to become an island of exaggerated importance. During my career on the screen, I have commanded excellent salaries, some admiration, fan mail, and a reputation—and my world contracted into not much more than a sound stage, my home, and occasional nights on the town. The circle of my friends closed in. The demands of my work—sometimes as much as fourteen hours a day—cut me off even from my brother Neil, who lived within half a mile of my apartment.

"I began to feel like a shut-in invalid, nursed by publicity. I have always liked space, the feeling of freedom, a broad range of friends, and variety (not excluding the publication). Now I had become a semi-automaton 'creating' a character another had written, doing what still another person told me to do on the set. Seeing the rushes, I could barely believe the colored shadow on the screen was myself.

"Possibly this was the reason I decided to find the rest of me. I loved three things: drama, politics, and sports, and I'm not sure they always come in that order. In all three of them I came out of the monastery of movies into the world . . . ."

On Dec. 7, 1941, the Japanese bombed Pearl Harbor and the world was never again the same for millions of young Americans, including Ronald Reagan.

Chapter Five

FORT ROACH

King's Row had not yet been released and Ronald Reagan had been collecting his new "star" salary of $3500 a week for less than three months when an envelope stamped, "Immediate Action Active Duty," arrived.

The war interrupted a career which had left "B" pictures far behind. In the 1940-41 season, Ronald Reagan was chosen in the movie exhibitors' poll, "Stars of Tomorrow," as one of five new players most likely to emerge as stars. At Warner Brothers, Reagan surged into second place in studio fan mail, according to an article in the Los Angeles *Times,* dated Dec. 2, 1941. The 30-year-old actor ranked second only to Errol Flynn, replacing James Cagney as runner up.

When he took his physical examination, the doctors demanded to know how he had passed the eye test years before. "If we sent you overseas, you'd shoot a general," one exclaimed. "Yes, and you'd miss him," replied another. Reagan confessed that he had tricked the examining officer years before. He was inducted but his papers were stamped, "No combat duty."

His first assignment (he was inducted April 14, 1942) was Fort Mason, San Francisco, as a liaison officer loading convoys. Although he tried to stick to the business of cargo and shipping dates, Lieutenant Reagan found himself constantly called upon to perform various show business "duties." First there was an interview with a San Francisco movie columnist, followed by bond rallies and charity benefits. *King's Row* came to the post theater and the young officer was introduced and asked to say a few words. Lieutenant Reagan was next called to Hollywood to appear at a giant rally of film stars launching the brand new USO (United Service Organizations).

The Monday following the rally, Fort Mason's commanding general called in the young officer to have a little chat about military priorities in a war. Reagan, who had been bothered by the flood of requests, quickly expressed *his* dissatisfaction as well and asked permission to refer all future invitations to the General's office which could then assign him as it saw fit. The General, who had been ready to lay down a heavy barrage, decided to hold his fire and before the meeting was over had promised Reagan his office would do what he had suggested. It was a small but significant incident. Reagan had met and overcome a difficult situation by being honest and himself. It is his invariable practice to this day.

A short while later, Lieutenant Reagan was transferred from the Army to the Air Force and from Fort Mason to a special "base" outside Los Angeles. The Air Force was starting a motion picture unit and needed men experienced in film making.

Colonel Phillip Booker, Reagan's commanding officer at Fort Mason, overrode his young subordinate's doubts with the comment: "To tell you the truth, whether you're willing or not, you're going—

because in thirty-four years, this is the first time I've ever seen the Army make sense. This is putting a square peg in a square hole."

And so the "square" lieutenant returned to Hollywood. The unit soon located at the Hal Roach Studios, which quickly became known as "Fort Roach," and in more satirical circles, "Fort Wacky."

It was an unusual military installation, beyond doubt, but "from a motion picture standpoint," argues Reagan, "it added up to about two hundred million dollars worth of talent on the hoof. We would turn out training films and documentaries, and conduct a training school for combat camera crews. . . . I have yet to go out on a personal appearance without having at least several TV or news photographers tell me, after a press conference, they learned their trade in our combat camera school."

Fort Roach numbered 1300 men and officers. Reagan was appointed base adjutant, that is, administrative officer. He was promoted to captain but asked that his promotion to major be canceled. "Who was I," he asks, "to be a major for serving in California without ever hearing a shot fired in anger?"

Reagan is proud of the job performed by the men at Fort Roach, explaining that "the military has need of many things, in wartime especially, so there will always be a need for specialized posts . . . . None has ever been more successful in fulfilling its mission than was our wacky Hollywood stepchild. One of our thirty-minute training films cut the training period for aerial gunners by six weeks."

They also worked on two important classified

projects. The first concerned the destruction of the Nazi V-2 rocket launching sites at Peenemunde, Germany. The rockets were not only damaging the civilian morale in England but would have affected the Normandy invasion if they had continued to operate at full efficiency. Details of their location and construction were obtained. Exact replicas of the sites were built in Florida and experimental bombings were carried out to discover how best to destroy the rocket installations. Reagan's camera crews at Fort Roach filmed the raids.

"Day after day," remembers Reagan, "we sat in a projection room in Culver City and saw fantastic slow-motion films of huge bombs bouncing off these concrete buildings as if they were pebbles, until one day we saw on-screen, armor-piercing bombs dropped from low altitudes, going through the huge concrete walls as if through cheese. Those films were flown directly to the Eighth Air Force, and the launch sites were knocked out in time to postpone the V-2 launchings long enough for D-Day to take place on schedule."

More spectacular and important was the project which dealt with the front thousands of miles away in the Pacific. As American airplanes began to hit closer and closer to Japan, film experts at Fort Roach concluded that bomber crews could reduce their losses and improve their efficiency if they knew exactly where they were going before they arrived there.

On their own, without any orders from the Pentagon, the special effects men at Fort Wacky built a complete miniature of Tokyo. It filled a sound stage. They erected a crane and camera mount above the model city and photographed it, creating the on-screen effect of movies taken from an airplane flying at various heights and speeds.

A group of distinguished generals were invited to a "sneak preview" at the studios. Real scenes taken by planes flying over Tokyo were mixed in with scenes of the model. The generals were informed of the melange and challenged to tell which were which. Although several had flown over Tokyo they could not. "Skepticism turned to enthusiasm," says Reagan and before long the sound stage was put under 24-hour guard and all but qualified personnel were denied admission.

Additional models of other Japanese cities were constructed. The special effects men became so proficient that they could show a bomb run as seen through the bombsight and even portray what the target would look like in darkness or bad weather.

Reagan was the narrator of the bombing runs, the briefing officer if you will, and would describe the entire flight from the first sighting of the island target to the command, "Bombs away!" "We kept these simulated bomb runs so authentic," he recalls, "that following each raid, recon planes would fly their film from Saipan direct to us so that we could burn out portions of our target scene and put in the scars of the bombing. Our film then would always look exactly the way the target would appear to the crews going in on the next run."

Reagan argues that "only an outfit like ours could have accomplished this task. Here was the true magic of motion picture making. . . ."

As the war drew to a close, Captain Reagan experienced his first direct contact with civilian bureaucracy, which resulted in "the first crack in my staunch liberalism."

Because of its classified status, Fort Roach did not have civilian employees until the last year and a half of the war. But one day two Civil Service representatives appeared to inform the base's adjutant (Ronald Reagan) that civilians were on their way. Two weeks later, 250 civilians arrived.

Fort Roach's military personnel section—responsible for 1300 men—was half the size of the personnel office that maintained the files of 250 civilians. "Their rules and regulations," Reagan says, "filled shelves from floor to ceiling, around virtually four walls of a barrack-sized building."

In his autobiography, Reagan tells the story of an officer-writer who came storming into his office one day, declaring he had to have a new secretary. The one assigned him by civilian personnel couldn't spell "cat"! When informed of the officer's request, the civilian personnel director calmly replied that there was no problem. She would simply draw up the papers and the officer would "sign the charges."

When the suspicious officer asked her to explain what she meant, the personnel director said that there would have to be a trial during which the officer would take "the stand in (his secretary's) presence and establish her incompetence."

Repelled by such procedure the officer refused to sign a complaint. Captain Reagan, by now familiar with Civil Service, inquired if there wasn't possibly any other way of solving the officer's problem.

As he suspected, the personnel director was ready with the perfect bureaucratic solution: she would transfer a qualified secretary to the officer and move the girl who couldn't spell "cat" to another office and a *better* job, thereby pleasing everyone and upsetting no one.

"So," Reagan has written, "the incompetent wound up with a promotion and a raise in pay. No one in the administrative hierarchy of Civil Service will ever interfere with this upgrading process because his own pay and rating are based on the number of employees beneath him and grades of those employees.

"It's a built-in process for empire building."

And it was to become a favorite theme of Ronald Reagan in the years ahead.

Chapter Six

STRIKES, COMMUNISTS AND A LOADED GUN

Serious strikes had begun in Hollywood even before the war's end as unions fought for jurisdiction of a $5 billion a year industry. Between 1945 and 1947, there were half a dozen major strikes in Hollywood, costing movie makers approximately $150 million. About 8,000 workers, it is estimated, lost nine million man hours and some $28 million in wages.

The bitter struggle was created to a great extent by Communist attempts to seize control of one of the most important media in the nation. Their role was not obvious, or even admitted, by many in Hollywood, including Ronald Reagan. At this time, Reagan was admittedly naive about communism. "I thought," he says, "the nearest Communists were fighting in Stalingrad." He also admits that he was a "near hopeless hemophilic liberal."

Following in his father's political footsteps, he had voted for Roosevelt all through the 1930's and 1940's. His army experience with civilian bureaucracy shook him but he still voted for Harry Truman in 1948, heading the Labor League of Hollywood Voters for him.

In fact, when he was discharged from the army at the end of 1945, his sympathies were unreservedly liberal, and his ambitions universal: "I would work with the tools I had: my thoughts, my speaking abilities, my reputation as an actor. I would try to bring about the regeneration of the world I believed should have automatically appeared" after World War Two. He joined every organization he could find "that would guarantee to save the world." (Among them were the United World Federalists and, later, Americans for Democratic Action.)

For over a year, he made speeches denouncing fascism to enthusiastic applause. Then one night, at the suggestion of a minister, he added a new last paragraph also denouncing communism. The audience sat sullen and silent and quite abruptly Reagan realized that the people he had been talking to were curiously one-minded.

He cut back drastically on his speaking engagements, especially for the American Veterans Committee, and started intense personal research on current affairs. He began to appreciate the very real menace of communism as he devoted more time to the Screen Actors Guild (SAG), of which he was a director, and its efforts to settle the still continuing jurisdictional strike.

Reagan had been appointed a member of the SAG board in 1941. For all of his adult life he has been a union man and stated in 1966 that "I . . . continue to be a strong believer in the rights of unions, as well as in the rights of individuals. I think we have the right as free men to refuse to work for just grievances: the strike is an inalienable weapon of any citizen."

SAG's efforts became all-important as violence increased. Autos were over-turned. Clubs, chains, bottles, bricks and two-by-four planks were used in scuffles between the warring unions. Homes of members were bombed and individuals were mugged.

Unable to look on passively any longer, SAG volunteered as a mediator and came close to finding a solution on several occasions. But each time its efforts failed, often at the very last moment. The reason why they failed was later revealed by congressional committees.

Both the House Committee on Un-American Activities of the U. S. Congress and the Senate Fact-Finding Committee on Un-American Activities of the California Legislature traced the strike to Communists. In 1959, the California committee reported:

"The Communist Party working in Hollywood wanted control over everything that moved on wheels . . . . They soon moved Communist units into those unions having jurisdiction over carpenters, painters, musicians, grips and electricians. To control these trade unions was to control the motion picture industry."

The strike, which was finally settled when responsible union leaders endorsed the position of the old-line International Alliance of Theatrical Stage Employees, had a profound effect on Ronald Reagan. He says, "I owe it to that period that I managed to sort out a lot of items in my personal life. From being an active (although unconscious) partisan in what now and then turned out to be Communist causes, I little by little became . . . awakened."

One man in particular who helped awaken him was film star George Murphy, a close friend, former president of the Screen Actors Guild and now U.S. Senator from California. Reminiscing in a room off the Senate floor in Washington, D. C., Senator Murphy told me:

"In those days I was interested in the activities and programs of the Communists to a greater degree than most of the fellows. I tried to explain to Ron but he thought I was trying to convince him he ought to be a Republican. Because of his involvement with labor he had automatically become involved with the Democratic party.

"Then later on he discovered what I had been trying to tell him and like all people who discover the faults of something they believe in very strongly, he swung around hard and became an active Republican—just as I did. You see, I had been a Democrat originally in 1939."

That Ronald Reagan evolved into a hard-hitting, effective anti-Communist was confirmed in 1951 in testimony before the House Committee on Un-American Activities when actor Sterling Hayden confessed his involvement in the Communist plot. Testifying on Communist maneuvers to capture Hollywood, Hayden was asked what stopped them. His answer: We "ran into the Board of Directors of the SAG and particularly into Ronald Reagan, who was a one-man battalion."

The prize which the Communists sought was worth more than all the booty sought by Kubla Khan. As Reagan pointed out years later, the Communists wanted the motion picture industry as a "world-wide propaganda base. In those days before television and massive foreign film production, American films dominated 95 per cent of the world's movie screens. We had a weekly audience of about 500,000,000 souls."

But the Communists were stopped by liberals

turned anti-communists like Ronald Reagan. One of his first experiences with Communists was their infiltration of the Hollywood branch of the American Veterans Committee, of which he was a national board member. Reagan worked hard for the AVC until one day he was told to report in full Air Corps uniform to picket a studio. He investigated the order and discovered that the action had been taken by a vote of 73 members out of a total of 1,300.

Reagan called headquarters to warn that if the picket was held as an official action of AVC membership, he would take full-page advertisements in the local newspapers denouncing it. In less than an hour the picket line was canceled. Shortly thereafter, in 1947, he resigned from the Hollywood chapter of the American Veterans Committee. "It had become," he wrote, "a hotbed of Communists in Hollywood, according to activities which were reported on by the California Senate Fact-Finding Committee on Un-American Activities. . . . Its reputation suffered so much that it had to be taken over in its entirety and cleansed by the national organization."

Another group which invited Ronald Reagan in 1946 to serve on its board was the Hollywood Independent Citizens Committee of Arts, Sciences and Professions (HICCASP), an ostensibly respectable and responsible organization. But when he attended his first board meeting, Reagan noted to his surprise the presence of several people with far-left and worse records.

The meeting proceeded smoothly until one board member rose to state that he was concerned as were several others about the persistent rumor that HICCASP was a Communist-front organization. He suggested the board clear the air by issuing a statement repudiating communism.

Reagan enthusiastically supported the suggestion, only to be bombarded with such epithets as "capitalist scum," "enemy of the proletariat," and "fascist."

Those in favor of the anti-Communist statement met later that evening at the apartment of Olivia de Havilland. There Reagan was told that the whole thing had been staged to smoke out the "others." Reagan looked at Olivia: "I thought you were one," he said. Miss de Havilland murmured back: "I thought *you* were one."

They set to work drafting a statement, with Reagan writing the first draft on the back of an envelope. The final version ended: "We reaffirm our belief in free enterprise and the democratic system and repudiate communism." When this statement was submitted for a vote to the members of a special HICCASP executive committee, it received one favorable ballot, that of Olivia de Havilland.

Reagan resigned from the board by telegram that night, as did others. Shortly thereafter, HICCASP folded.

As a result of this and other anti-Communist activity, Reagan began receiving threats against his life. One night, on location, he was called to a phone where an unidentified voice told him: "There's a group being formed to deal with you. They're going to fix you so you won't ever act again."

The next day, at the insistence of friends and associates, Warner Brothers Studios arranged for the police to issue Reagan a license to carry a gun. He

STRIKES, COMMUNISTS, A LOADED GUN 57

wore a loaded .32 Smith & Wesson revolver in a shoulder holster for months.

What convinced him to keep wearing it was the story told him that "They" were scoffing at such precautions: "This is all cooked up nonsense," they were reported as saying. "If we had wanted to throw acid in Reagan's face, we would have done it, not talked about it."

As the actor wrote: "No one had mentioned acid-throwing—up to that revealing moment."

During this turbulent period, Ronald Reagan was elected president of the 15,000 member Screen Actors Guild, succeeding Robert Montgomery. He was elected president a total of six times—more than any other prexy. He also served on SAG's board of directors for 16 years. He received many awards for his union activities, including a certificate from the American Newspaper Guild (CIO) in 1952, praising him for "spearheading the fight against Communism in Hollywood." He was also cited by the AFL Auto Workers Union.

Under his leadership, the SAG purged its ranks of actors who were not cleared of Communist charges. SAG later adopted as official policy the condemnation of all members "who have been named as past or present Communist party members and in appearing before the House Committee on Un-American Activities refused to state whether they are or ever have been members of the Party."

The Guild also declared that any applicant for membership must sign the following statement: "I am not now and will not become a member of the Communist Party or of any other organization that seeks to overthrow the government of the United States by force and violence."

In summing up these long months of struggle against the Communists, Reagan has written: "We fought on the issues and proved that if you keep the people informed on those issues, they won't make a mistake."

He has always had great confidence in the people and great mistrust of any attempts to control or manage them. In May, 1947, he said:

"Our highest aim should be the cultivation of freedom of the individual, for therein lies the highest dignity of man. Tyranny is tyranny and—whether it comes from the Right, Left or Center—it is evil. I suspect the Extreme Right and the Extreme Left of political ideologies, though seeming to branch off in opposite directions, curve to a common meeting point.

"I believe the only logical way to save our country from both extremes is to remove conditions that supply fuel for the totalitarian fire."

Reagan's administrative ability was recognized again in 1949 when he was elected chairman of the Motion Picture Industry Council, which represents 35,000 members of nine major acting, labor and management groups, and is the film capital's most prestigious organization. He served for 10 years on the Council's board of directors.

His duties as SAG president were many and demanding. Following settlement of the strike in 1947, he was called to Washington, D.C. to appear before the House Committee on Un-American Activities. There he testified about Communist infiltration of Hollywood and reiterated his faith in democracy, saying:

"I would hesitate, or not like, to see any political party outlawed on the basis of ideology. We have spent 170 years in this country on the basis that democracy is strong enough to stand up and fight against the inroads of any ideology. However, if it is proven that an organization is an agent of a power, a foreign power or in any way not a legitimate political party, and I think the government is capable of proving that, if the proof is there, then that is another matter."

Ronald Reagan was and is a man who is steadfastly against giving *any* government, federal, state or local, too much power, whatever the reason. In his testimony before the House Committee on Un-American Activities, he said that he detested and abhorred communism and its "fifth column" tactics, but added, "At the same time I never as a citizen want to see our country become urged, by either fear or resentment of this group, that we ever compromise with any of our democratic principles through that fear or resentment."

One of those principles is the right of dissent which he exercised in 1959 by refusing to attend a party given by 20th Century Fox for visiting Soviet Premier Nikita Khrushchev.

As SAG President, he also testified in Los Angeles before a special sub-committee of the House Committee on Education and Labor. The two-year film strike consumed hundreds of hours of Ronald Reagan's time, as did normal negotiations about wages and working conditions of SAG members. He concedes that his long association with the Screen Actors Guild hurt his movie career, but he has a typical explanation:

"I think I became too identified with the serious side of Hollywood's off-screen life—there were too many people who saw me only as a committee member. Would I do it again? Yes—this has been the best of all possible lives for me and I think you have to do something to pay your way in life."

Taft Schreiber, his agent for 30 years and now vice-president of the giant entertainment company, MCA, corroborates Reagan's deep-rooted belief in public service. "(He) was not at a point in his life when he needed the Union activities to make personal progress—he had a substantial contract, had achieved stability and permanence for himself in the industry, and it was rare that anyone as young and as involved in screen work would give of himself to the extent required, for it meant negotiating, and giving many extra curricular hours to this responsibility that only the most dedicated would choose to undertake."

Unfortunately for his career, he did so well as SAG head that his fellow actors elected him again and again as their president. *Life* magazine has commented: "Reagan was an extremely capable labor leader and the guild's esteem for him is evidenced by the fact that he was recalled to the union presidency in a 1959 emergency, to lead a successful strike against the studios over the issue of TV residual pay for actors."

That same year, 1959, he testified in Washington on behalf of the Screen Actors Guild in favor of tax-cut legislation. After criticizing the theory of progressive taxation, he took the opportunity, as he usually did, to describe the American dream, waxing so eloquent that Rep. John Byrnes of Wisconsin was moved to comment:

"May I make a comment that I think Mr. Reagan ought to run for Congress because we need more of his philosophy and persuasiveness here in Congress."

In Reagan's own mind, the most important dividend of his union presidency was a meeting in

STRIKES, COMMUNISTS, A LOADED GUN 61

1951 with a lovely 27-year-old actress named Nancy Davis. He met Nancy, the daughter of a famed Chicago neuro-surgeon, Loyal Davis, after director Mervyn Le Roy had asked the SAG president to help a young MGM actress. It seemed that the young lady's name kept appearing on Communist front rosters and she was receiving notices about pro-Communist meetings she had no intention of attending. After a quick check which revealed that the young lady was a very vocal anti-Communist, Reagan decided to reassure the young actress in person—over an early dinner. The small (5'4") girl with the wide brown eyes so intrigued the union head that the evening did not end until 3:30 a.m.

Nancy was a graduate of Girls Latin School in Chicago and Smith College and came by her interest in acting familially—her mother appeared on Broadway as Edith Luckett. She came to Hollywood, after some summer stock with such stars as Zasu Pitts, "because acting offered a different way of life. I didn't want to go back to Chicago and lead the life of a sub-deb."

Nancy's father is past president of such organizations as the American Surgical Association, the American College of Surgeons and the Society of Neurological Surgeons. A well-known and articulate conservative, Dr. Davis has edited a number of medical journals and textbooks. He was largely responsible for his daughter's anti-communism, which matched so well the viewpoint of the SAG president.

Recalls Nancy, "Ronnie made me aware of all that was going on. That was one of the first things that impressed me and attracted me to him. He had so many other interests beside the film business.

I can't remember him talking about his last picture. He had such a fund of knowledge—he could talk about horses, wine, books, politics. He's the best story-teller I ever heard."

Ron and Nancy dated for over a year before it finally dawned on him (at a SAG meeting) that they ought to get married—which they did on March 4, 1952, at the Little Brown Church in the Valley in North Hollywood, with William Holden as best man, and Mrs. Holden as the matron of honor. Nancy stopped acting (she had appeared in eight films), explaining that "if you try to make two careers work, one of them has to suffer. Maybe some women can do it, but not me." They have two children, Patricia Ann, born in 1953, and Ronald Prescott, born in 1958.

For a number of reasons, good pictures now came less frequently. Reagan was so busy with SAG business that producers now typecast him as an off-screen rather than on-screen personality.

Second, the public no longer depended exclusively on movies for its entertainment: television was beginning to cast its flickering shadow across the nation and on Hollywood.

Third, in Reagan's words, "my Air Corps chores had exposed me to the Monday morning conversation of a lot of Civil Service stenographers, average age eighteen, and they weren't 'oohing and aahing' over Robert Taylor, Jimmy Stewart, or Tyrone Power, let alone me. Their age group was about sixty per cent of the movie audience and they had come to ticket-buying age while all of us were off-screen. They had a new set of heroes."

Finally, there were a couple of serious illnesses which interrupted a film career already in shadow because of intense Screen Actors Guild activity.

One night, for example, Ronald Reagan went to a premiere at the Carthay Circle Theater, but before the evening was out he was in Cedars of Lebanon Hospital with a brand of virus pneumonia, on which miracle drugs had no effect. Reagan was desperately sick for weeks and remembers one night when he almost decided to stop breathing. An anonymous nurse persuaded him to take one more breath and then another and "she was so nice and persistent that I let her have her way."

Reagan's agent then negotiated a new contract with Warner's which gave the actor the right to do outside pictures: he was now free lance. Universal Pictures immediately signed him up for five pictures in five years, the first one a crime film with top actress Ida Lupino. On the Sunday before the first day's shooting, June 19, 1949, Reagan played as usual in a baseball game benefiting the City of Hope Hospital. "Before the end of the first inning, I was lying just off first base with a comminuted multiple fracture of my right thigh." He was in traction for two months, and underwent a year of therapy before his leg would support him and his knee recovered about 85 per cent of its normal resiliency.

With bills piling up and on his own as a freelance actor, Ronald Reagan had two choices: take whatever came along to get ahead financially or wait for the right part in the right picture. The Reagans decided to ride out the rough weather. For 14 months, he turned down every script offered him for the simplest of all reasons: they were terrible. He also told MCA, which was now handling him, that both Broadway and a television series were on the "won't do" list. Reagan was opposed to a TV series because, in his opinion, the actors in it were forever afterward identified with those roles.

MCA suggested a nightclub act in Las Vegas, and Reagan reluctantly agreed. He appeared at The Last Frontier "for a wonderfully successful two weeks, with a sellout every night and offers from the Waldorf in New York and top clubs from Miami to Chicago." But the Reagans decided that two weeks were enough and went home to ride and raise horses, and cattle too, on their 370 acre ranch in the Malibu Hills. The ranch, purchased in 1952, was named Yearling Row.

And, then, at last, came the "part" which was to give him a brand new career in a new medium —and complete his political transformation from liberal Democrat to conservative Republican.

Chapter Seven

A RENDEZVOUS WITH DESTINY

General Electric was looking for a new television program, something that would last. Revue Productions, a subsidiary of MCA, thought it had the answer: a weekly dramatic series featuring top Hollywood stars with Ronald Reagan as the host and lead in half a dozen plays each year. What made the proposal so unusual and attractive was that off-screen Reagan would make personal appearances at GE's plants and in selected communities as part of the company's Employee and Community Relations Program. Was Reagan interested? He certainly was. So was General Electric.

In the fall of 1954, *GE Theater* began an eight-year run "with more 'firsts' to its credit than anything on television before or since," boasts its host. Among them were (a) the first series to emanate from both New York and Hollywood, and (b) the first series to alternate between live and filmed shows. For seven of the eight years, *GE Theater* ranked first in a prime spot—nine o'clock Sunday night.

"Our secret wasn't any secret at all," says Reagan; "we tried for variety and quality in our stories, and we cast with the best we could get—particularly from the world of motion pictures. In our eight years we starred half a hundred Academy Award winners—many made their first, and some their only, television appearance on our show."

GE Theater made Ronald Reagan a star in the most important medium in the nation. It brought him financial security with an annual salary of $120,000, which finally reached $165,000 when he became part owner of the series. And it put him on the road for GE from coast to coast, talking to people in 31 different states. Reagan has estimated that in those eight years he visited all 135 GE plants and personally met every one of its 250,000 employees. "Two of the eight years were spent traveling, and with speeches sometimes running at fourteen a day, I was on my feet in front of a 'mike' for about 250,000 minutes."

He got to know these employees, ordinary every day citizens like most of us, and he is fond of remarking that too many political leaders "have underestimated them." He is convinced, reflecting this conviction today, that "they want the truth. . . . They are concerned, not with security as some would have us believe, but with their very firm personal liberties."

He worked hard. At one plant he autographed ten thousand photographs in two days. At another, he stood in a receiving line and shook two thousand hands. At a plant in Louisville, Ky., he walked miles of assembly line twice, once for the day shift and a second time for the night shift. He recalls punningly: "No barnstorming politician ever met the people on quite such a common footing."

The community relations part of his job started more slowly but in a few months he was talking to dozens of civic and educational organizations about

Hollywood, the *real* Hollywood. The most dramatic section of his remarks dealt with the attempted takeover of the film industry by the Communists. Reagan was dumbfounded to discover how "completely uninformed the average audience was concerning internal Communism and how it operated." He determined to educate them, and in the process, his speeches began to concentrate more and more on communism *and* collectivism. "The Hollywood portion of the talk shortened and disappeared," he admits. "The warning words of what could happen changed to concrete examples of what has already happened, and I learned very early to document those examples."

That "I" comes naturally. In an age of omnipresent ghosts and speech-writers, Ronald Reagan researches and writes his own speeches. He is particularly proud of two awards he has received: Freedom Foundation Awards in 1960 and 1962 for "outstanding achievement in bringing about a better understanding of the American way of life."

His addresses during the 1950's and early 1960's were carefully non-partisan. He emphasized that the problem of centralized power in Washington cut across political lines and that government could grow so large that it usurped the policy-making functions of *all* parties.

From the very first, he was well-received. Speaking invitations poured into General Electric offices. When *GE Theater* went off the air in 1962, speaking tours had to be canceled as far ahead as 1966. Reagan modestly explains the overwhelming reception:

"I think the real reason had to do with a change that was taking place all over America. People wanted to talk about and hear about encroaching government control, and hopefully they wanted suggestions as to what they themselves could do to turn the tide."

They also wanted to hear someone who spoke with so much conviction and urgency about what was happening to them and their country.

Earl Dunkel, the General Electric representative who first accompanied Reagan on his travels, remembers that the actor had "an almost mystical ability to achieve an empathy with almost any audience." Now a top executive with the company, Dunkel says that Reagan was able to talk on *any* subject, for example education, and persuade a group of educators that he must have had his training in that area. And "in those days he spoke totally off the cuff—not even note cards."

He was unusually thoughtful about others, recalls Dunkel, who tells this story:

"In Erie, Pa., one night we came back to the hotel so dog-tired all we wanted was to go right to bed. But there was a young girl who had been sitting in the lobby for four hours, waiting. She wanted to be an actress. She had all the posturings of the would-be actress. Ronnie was a hero from out of the screen-play magazines and she wanted to know what to do. And this man, dog-tired as he was, recognizing that this little girl was going just the wrong route sat down in that lobby with her for an hour and a half, explaining what to do if she were really serious. His advice was to do things right there in Erie, Pa.—get on radio, get on television, get in the little theater—pointing out that if she could win an audience in Erie, she could win an audience anywhere."

He was far less vain than a celebrity has a right

to be, insists Dunkel, who remembers that when they arrived at the usual two-bedroom hotel suite he and Reagan would flip a coin, with the winner getting the big room and the loser the small one.

George Dalen succeeded Earl Dunkel and was to accompany Reagan around the country, north, south, east and west, for nearly seven years. He too remembers the actor's non-prima donna behavior:

"We boarded a pullman* late one night to head back to New York from Rhode Island. We were somewhat disconcerted on awakening to find that we were still in the yards at Providence. A driving snow storm had stalled the trains. . . .

"Since this was a night train, there was naturally, no food service aboard. We had with us a box of jellybeans which Reagan regularly carried on these jaunts and a couple bags of popcorn we had picked up in the station the night before. The porter on the train had a thermos of coffee.

"As we discussed our mutual plight, the three of us sat down in the porter's quarters and shared jellybeans, popcorn and the porter's coffee which was sufficient to sustain us to New York. Here again, it was not a question of making a gesture —it was just the natural and human thing to do, so he did it."

That he liked people can be seen from this listing of the varied groups he would meet on a "typical" day: "a press conference breakfast; G.E. employees ranging from secretarial, management,

* Reagan grounded himself after World War II, and thereafter traveled exclusively by train or car until 1965 when he again began to fly, explaining, "I think I have to be willing to do whatever the job (of governor) requires, particularly in the line of travel."

shop workers, and professional engineers and technical people; G.E. distributors and dealers; city fathers; women's clubs' administrative associations; plus others, as well as speaking to Chamber of Commerce, Kiwanis, Rotary, school groups, et cetera."

Dalen makes the telling point that while Reagan attracted attention as a Hollywood star, he *retained* people's interest because he was "so articulate and well-informed."

Sometimes, however, he ran into opposition. In 1959, he was scheduled to speak at a Los Angeles convention when a GE officer informed him that a Federal government official had protested to the company about Reagan's proposed speech. He planned to use the Tennessee Valley Authority (TVA) as an example of how government programs can expand beyond their original purpose. It was suggested, Reagan recounts, that he be fired and pointed references were made to the millions of dollars worth of business that GE did with the Federal government every year.

Reagan asked how Ralph Cordiner, GE's president, had reacted. Cordiner, he was told, had said that GE "would not tell any individual what he could not say," and that Cordiner would handle the matter personally.

The government official was incredulous, but GE stood firm. However, Reagan began to wonder whether he had "carte blanche" to say whatever he wanted—and jeopardize so much business for his sponsor. Reagan decided to call Cordiner in New York. The GE chairman stated that he was sorry that Reagan had learned about the affair, that "it's my problem and I've taken it on." Reagan responded by saying that he wouldn't want to think GE might have to fire several thousand men because of what he said. Cordiner did not pick up the hint. Finally, Reagan realized it was up to him:

"Mr. Cordiner," he asked, "what would you say if I said I could make my speech just as effectively without mentioning TVA?"

After a long pause, the reply came: "Well, it would make my job easier."

Reagan recounts: "Dropping TVA from the speech was no problem. You can reach out blindfolded and grab a hundred examples of overgrown government. The whole attempt only served to illustrate how late it is if we are to save freedom."

It also served to illustrate that Big Business is not always ready to abandon principle for a piece of the Federal pork barrel.

One of our nation's outstanding businessmen, Ralph Cordiner has tremendous respect for Reagan and his ability to establish rapport with either large or small audiences. "I think," he told this writer, "the listening and viewing audience is impressed with his sincerity, his thoughtfulness and his forthrightness." The former chief executive of General Electric is also struck by Reagan's unusual habit, for so busy a man, of personally studying a subject. "Ronald Reagan is a student," he says, "and does not appear before an audience, write a speech, deliver a paper or even have a discussion with a very small group unless he has researched and reviewed the subject before the group for consideration." The actor, he emphasizes, was a "unanimous" choice as host of the *GE Theater* and as "a spokesman, not for the Company, but for what he personally thought were the important issues and some of the basic truths that many of us knew during boyhood or an earlier period, and which apparently were presently being forgotten or ignored."

Ronald Reagan was involved in other incidents that revealed the changing times and his changing personality. One night, he was scheduled to speak in St. Paul, Minnesota, at an assembly at Central High School. But when he arrived he was greeted by the news that the Teachers Federation had passed a resolution the night before demanding that Ronald Reagan not be allowed to address the students because he was a "controversial personality." (This was several years after the end of the alleged Reign of Terror carried out by Senator Joseph McCarthy of Wisconsin.)

That morning Reagan stepped out onto the stage of the high school auditorium not knowing how the students would react. He needn't have worried. They gave him a five-minute standing ovation. "They damn well didn't want someone telling them," Reagan says, "whom they could or couldn't listen to."

The next night in Minneapolis, just across the river, where Reagan was the banquet speaker, a St. Paul teacher asked to say a few words to the audience. He proceeded to make a public apology on behalf of the St. Paul teachers for the anti-Reagan resolution. Reagan later learned from a reporter that only a handful of teachers out of a membership of 1200 had attended the meeting at which the resolution was passed.

Reagan's early experience as a labor negotiator and battler against the Communists now stood him in good stead. As he became more and more determined and more and more effective, the attacks increased in ferocity.

At last, he received the inevitable decoration of every effective conservative and/or anti-Communist: an attack by Drew Pearson. Early one morning, in his California home, Reagan was awakened by a Pearson assistant and asked about his views on Medicare. As he says: "Somehow my answers must not have weathered the trip from Los Angeles by phone to Washington, and through Pearson's typewriter, because they came out turned around in a vitriolic attack against me and the American Medical Association. It made it easier to understand why three United States presidents of both parties had publicly questioned his tactics."

For seven years, Sunday night at nine belonged to the General Electric's dramatic series. But in television, even the top-rated shows eventually lose favor and the *GE Theater* at last met its match in the eighth year—a cowboy spectacular called *Bonanza*. It wasn't a real contest: "Our half-hour, black and white, was up against an hour color program with four permanent stars, plus a weekly guest star, all wrapped up in a budget several millions of dollars greater than ours."

Another factor in GE's decision to cancel the show was the activities of the host and their company representative. Ronald Reagan was no longer just a Hollywood and television star. His activities had become increasingly political. In 1960, he campaigned openly for Richard Nixon's presidential candidacy. "I literally traveled," he recalls, "the same kind of campaign route the candidate himself traveled—all over the country." It was not a halfhearted commitment: Reagan made over 200 speeches for Nixon as a Democrat.*

In 1962, when Nixon ran for governor of California, Reagan again took to the hustings, this time as a Republican. He says, "I didn't want to become a professional Democrat for Republican candidates and I registered as a Republican in January, 1962." Later that year, he served as honorary campaign chairman for Loyd Wright, a staunch conservative and distinguished lawyer, in the Republican primary against incumbent Senator Thomas Kuchel, an equally undiluted liberal. Kuchel, who won handily, repaid Reagan in kind in 1966 by supporting the actor's opponent, George Christopher, in the GOP gubernatorial primary.

Another candidate the actor "campaigned" for in 1962 was Representative John Rousselot, a prominent member of the John Birch Society, who had been elected to Congress in 1960. Reagan critics have tried to magnify this political coupling out of all proportion. Here are the facts: On Aug. 30 Reagan traveled to Pasadena to speak at a $50-a-plate fund-raising affair for Rousselot. That was the total extent of his campaigning for the Congressman except as Reagan says, "I urged in my

* Ten years before, he supported Congresswoman Helen Gahagan Douglas when she ran against then Congressman Richard Nixon for the U.S. Senate from California. Although he has been described as having campaigned actively for Mrs. Douglas, Reagan told me, "I don't actually recall ever doing anything particularly for her as an individual. But as a Democrat I supported the ticket from top to bottom." In answer to a detailed letter of mine, Mrs. Douglas simply replied, "Ronald Reagan supported my campaign for the Senate in 1950. At that time, he was a Democrat." The 1950 campaign was to be the last one in which he supported the Democratic ticket *in toto*. In 1952, Reagan backed Dwight Eisenhower for President.

talks the voting of a solid ticket. If you send the general, you send the troops with him."

He did not abandon acting by any means. In 1964, he signed up as host and occasional star of the television series, *Death Valley Days*, beginning its 13th season. He also began making movies again: a remake of Ernest Hemingway's *The Killers* was released in 1964. Despite his forays into politics in 1960 and 1962, Ronald Reagan seemed to be settling into the comfortable routine of a successful Hollywood and television star in middle age. He and Nancy and the two children were happy in their handsome, $100,000 home in the Los Angeles suburb of Pacific Palisades overlooking the Pacific Ocean. On weekends and often during the week, they would retreat to their ranch, Yearling Row, where Reagan would ride his favorite mount, a dapple gray named Nancy D.* There were cookouts in dungarees with old friends like the Robert Taylors. As they always had, the Reagans shunned the restaurant-night club-premiere life of Hollywood.

However, Ronald Reagan continued to speak across the country and he continued to discover that what he said received perceptibly more partisan reactions.

"It's a curious thing," he wrote in his autobiography in 1965; "I talked on this theme of big government during six years of the Eisenhower administration and was accepted as presenting a nonpartisan viewpoint. The same speech delivered *after* Jan. 20, 1961, brought down thunders of

* In 1966, a few days before Election Day, he sold the ranch to 20th Century Fox for a reported $2 million, retaining the right to use the ranch until the film studio formally moved there.

wrath on my mind, the charge that my speech was a partisan political attack, an expression of right wing extremism. My erstwhile associates in organized labor at the top level of the AFL-CIO assail me as a 'strident voice of the right wing lunatic fringe.' Sadly I have come to realize that a great many so-called liberals aren't liberal—they will defend to the death your right to agree with them."

He concluded what a large number of political philosophers have come to admit, "the labels somehow have got pasted on the wrong people.

"The conservatives believe the collective responsibility of the qualified men in a community should decide its course. The liberals believe in remote and massive strong-arming from afar, usually Washington, D.C. The conservatives believe in the unique powers of the individual and his personal opinions. The liberals lean increasingly toward bureaucracy, operation by computer minds and forced fiat, the submergence of man in statistics . . . .

"It is a fascinating phenomenon of our times. One of change, certainly; perhaps degeneracy. Our weaknesses have overnight become strengths."

Many public figures, including Senator Barry Goldwater of Arizona, were making the same analysis and sounding the same warning but few equaled Reagan's ability to simplify and dramatize the philosophical change taking place. It seemed obvious to many people, and a growing number of politicians, that the actor's real place was not Hollywood, but Sacramento or Washington, D.C. This was not a new thought: Democrats had attempted to persuade Ronald Reagan to run for Congress in the late Forties—against Congressman Donald Jackson, a member, of all things, of the House Committee on Un-American Activities. Reagan rejected the Democratic offer. He was approached in 1962 to run for either the Republican gubernatorial or Senatorial nomination, but turned both down, campaigning strenuously for Nixon. In 1964, he was again approached by Republicans, this time about the Senatorial nomination. He again declined and his old friend, George Murphy, was tapped to run against Pierre Salinger, beating the former press secretary to John F. Kennedy in a major upset. So it might have continued for years, with his conscience gnawing at him but he not knowing exactly how to still it. But then, in the fall of 1964, he made The Speech.

Ronald Reagan and Barry Goldwater had been good friends for many years (the Reagan family vacations every year in Phoenix—Goldwater's home town) and when Goldwater was nominated for President it was the most natural of appointments for Reagan to become co-chairman of California Citizens for Goldwater-Miller. Once again, as he had done for Nixon, he hit the "sawdust trail," made speeches, attended fund-raising events and impressed the voters of California. A late October telecast revealed nationally what a lot of Californians already knew: Ronald Reagan was a natural politician.

The broadcast came late in the campaign, on Tuesday evening, October 27, only one week before Election Day. Senator Goldwater's campaign manager, Denison Kitchel, and the Senator's single most important backroom advisor, William Baroody, had read the script of the proposed telecast and were against it. It was too "emotional" and "un-scholarly," they agreed. And it referred to social security in such a negative way that it was certain, they insisted, to stir up public fears once again about Barry Goldwater's views on social security. Here is the passage that so concerned Baroody and the others:

"Now are we so lacking in business sense that we cannot put this (Social Security) program on a sound actuarial basis, so that those who do depend on it won't come to the cupboard and find it bare, and at the same time can't we introduce voluntary features so that those who can make better provisions for themselves are allowed to do so? Incidentally, we might also allow participants in Social Security to name their own beneficiaries, which they cannot do in the present program. These are not insurmountable problems."

Dangerous and negative, concluded Baroody and the others. But they were in a dilemma. They had bought a half-hour of prime television time and they had to fill it with *something*. Someone suggested a rerun of a program called "Brunch with Barry," which featured the Senator and a half-dozen ladies talking about high prices and the war in Vietnam. "Brunch with Barry" had been well received when it was first viewed and was effective enough in a low-key way. But it was scarcely the blockbuster of a program urgently needed in the fading days of a national campaign.

A call came in from California, less than three hours before show-time. The chairman of the Goldwater TV Committee stated politely but firmly that Baroody and Kitchel had better okay the Reagan telecast—or find the money for their

A RENDEZVOUS WITH DESTINY

program. The TV Committee would *not* release funds for any other show. Faced with this ultimatum, Baroody reluctantly granted permission for showing the television program which was to make political history.

The next morning, a flood of telegrams, letters and telephone calls hit the Republican National Committee, lauding the Reagan show and asking for a repeat. The program was shown again nationally the following Saturday night and was telecast hundreds of times by state, county and local Goldwater committees.

"A Time for Choosing," as it was called, shifted tens of thousands of votes.[1] It raised about $600,000 for the national campaign through a brief plea for funds which ended the program. It was called the "one bright spot in a dismal campaign" by *Time* magazine. It prompted more than a few people to wonder what would have happened in 1964 if Reagan had been on the national ticket. And, it made Ronald Reagan a national political "star" overnight.[2]

The Speech embodies all of Reagan's very best qualities. It is filled with facts and specifics. It has humor. It takes firm stands based on principles. It is dramatic, poetic, and profoundly moving. Reagan delivered it superbly, not simply because he is a trained speaker and actor, but because he believed it, and had believed it for many years. It was not a script he was handed to study and memorize a few days before the broadcast. It was the product of his own thinking and research, it was the essence

[1] A complete text can be found in the Appendix.
[2] Nellie Reagan was not there to share her son's triumph, having died in 1962.

of his philosophy which had crystallized and matured years before and which now received its first national exposure. The results were electric and its concluding sentences were prophetic, especially for the man who uttered them:

"You and I have a rendezvous with destiny. We can preserve for our children this the last best hope of man on earth or we can sentence them to take the first step into a thousand years of darkness. If we fail, at least let our children and our children's children say of us we justified our brief moment here. We did all that could be done."

PART TWO

THE CANDIDATE

Chapter Eight

THE *ONLY* CANDIDATE

In late February of 1965 a group of influential leaders in the California Republican Party called on Ronald Reagan. Among them were A. C. (Cy) Rubel, former head of Union Oil Company; Henry Salvatori, chairman of the Western Geophysical Company of America, and Holmes Tuttle, one of the biggest auto distributors in Los Angeles. All were conservatives, all had raised millions of dollars for the GOP, and all were tired of losing elections. They came right to the point:

"Ron," they said, in essence, "we think you are the only candidate around whom the party can rally in the 1966 gubernatorial race. We think you can win and we are willing to underwrite your 'campaigning' for the rest of the year. Travel around the state, find out for yourself whether you are acceptable to the Party and if you are, *run*."

At first Reagan said flatly, "No." Then at their insistence, he agreed to think it over. He was very skeptical. He had never seriously considered running for public office. He had turned down similar offers in 1962 and 1964. He knew that the nomination contest and the general election afterwards would demand more of him than anything he had ever done before. After all, he had always campaigned for someone else—never himself. But so many people now insisted that *he* run. The preceding November, Frank Jordan, California's Secretary of State and the only Republican to hold state-wide office, had publicly declared, "I would certainly like to see Reagan run for governor." The actor himself had admitted in the same month that the mail reaction to his national telecast for Barry Goldwater had exceeded anything else in his career. It was causing him, he added, to give some "second thoughts" to his political future. Finally, after many talks with his wife Nancy, and ensuing sleepless nights, he told the group that he would run *provided* that he became convinced that the party would unite behind him. Political considerations were not his sole motivation. He also decided to run through that sense of duty which has always motivated him. He was determined not to be the cause of any intra-party squabbles such as had seriously weakened the party in 1958, 1962 and 1964. He also knew that a Republican can only win in California, with its 3-2 Democratic registration, with a united Republican party behind him. As he later explained, "I happen to feel very strongly that we have reached a period in which the philosophical differences between the two parties are so great that it is high time that more people from the rank and file of the citizenry involve themselves, so that we can have government *of and by,* as well as for the people."

Why did these prominent Republicans think so highly of Reagan? Because in many ways, he was an ideal candidate for the giant, golden state of California.

THE *ONLY* CANDIDATE

(1) He had unquestioned charm and voter appeal, to men as well as women. As *Los Angeles* magazine stated: "He is one of those rare men whom other men can stomach even while large groups of women are adoring him."

(2) He lived in Los Angeles in the more populous southern half of the state. Nearly 40 per cent of the electorate resides in the greater Los Angeles area.

(3) He was assured of substantial financial backing, an absolute necessity in a state of over 19 million people and a coastline that stretches 840 miles.

(4) He would have organizational muscle: the same dedicated people who worked so hard for Barry Goldwater in California in 1964 could be depended upon to turn out for Reagan.

(5) As a former Democrat, he cut across party lines in a state where party loyalty had never been strong. Starting with Governor Hiram Johnson back in 1911, state-wide candidates invariably ran on their records and personalities.

(6) He was a master of television, the medium which is so important in the far-flung reaches of California.

(7) He had a name already known by millions of people through his movies and television series. (According to polls, he began the campaign with a 97 percent identity factor.)

(8) For all the Hollywood glow, Reagan was an earnest, intelligent man who projected these qualities in person or on the screen.

And George Murphy's Senatorial victory in 1964 showed that the "mere actor" charge was not very effective with California voters.

Finally, those who had studied his career knew

that he was blessed with that elusive quality ever present in winners—luck. In college, radio, Hollywood, business, television and politics, he was usually in the right place at the right time with the right answer.

The answer which he developed in the coming months for a badly divided Republican Party was: Let's work and win together. Let's stop pinning labels on each other, and start pinning back the ears of the opposition. It was just the right balm for California Republicans still aching and smarting from the deep wounds of the Goldwater versus Rockefeller presidential primary in 1964, the Dick Nixon versus Joseph Shell gubernatorial primary in 1962 and the William Knowland-Goodwin Knight-George Christopher debacle in 1958.

After three straight major defeats the party wanted a winner, and the small group of Republicans who came calling on Reagan in early 1965 aimed to oblige. They demonstrated their seriousness by enabling Reagan to hire the best political campaign firm in the state, Spencer-Roberts and Haffner of Los Angeles and San Francisco, to help Reagan. The signing up of this firm was most important—politically and psychologically.

Formed in 1960, Spencer-Roberts has compiled an impressive record of 41 victories out of 48 major political races. Among its clients have been Rep. John Rousselot (1960), Sen. Thomas Kuchel (1962), Representatives Del Clawson and Don Clausen (1962), Nelson Rockefeller (the 1964 Presidential primary) and several Los Angeles County Council candidates. They have been hired to run Sen. Thomas Kuchel's re-election campaign in 1968.

THE *ONLY* CANDIDATE

Spencer-Roberts does not handle Democrats but does service a wide variety of Republicans—excepting what they call "kooks." All Republicans are agreed that the firm is the number one political management outfit in California. (Barry Goldwater sought its expertise for the 1964 California primary but made a firm offer too late—a Rockefeller man was there first with a blank check.) Stu Spencer and Bill Roberts, both in their early forties, are indefatigable men who thrive on 18-hour days.

Reagan insisted to Rubel, Salvatori and Tuttle that he wanted the best professional help available. Spencer and Roberts met the actor for the very first time in April, 1965, at a Hollywood restaurant. A second meeting took place at Reagan's home in Pacific Palisades, with partner Fred Haffner of San Francisco participating. Most of the questions were asked by the three political pros. At a third meeting, held again at the prospective candidate's home in early May, Reagan asked most of the questions. Finally, there was nothing more to ask. The four men looked at each other and with smiles all around made a commitment to "go all the way if things went right."

Bill Roberts, who functioned as campaign director throughout 1965 and 1966, told me that Ronald Reagan "in all sincerity approached this thing with the idea he could help the Party and unify the Party. We thought so too. We also thought he could win."

With the skilled Spencer-Roberts team in his corner and solid financial backing, Ronald Reagan began traveling in the spring of 1965—packing houses and setting attendance records wherever he went. His charm, his articulateness and his candor captivated audiences from San Diego to Redding.

In June, 1965, a blue-chip citizens committee was formed, called "Friends of Ronald Reagan," to demonstrate wide-spread party support for his impending candidacy. Its leadership included many of the top Republicans, liberal and conservative, in the state. Among them were:

(a) Cy Rubel, a delegate to the 1964 GOP National Convention, finance chairman for Joseph Shell in 1962 and a member of the Murphy for Senator Finance Committee in 1964.

(b) David Chow, an importer-exporter, who headed Chinese-American committees for Nixon in 1952, Goodwin Knight in 1954, and Kuchel in 1962.

(c) Philip Davis, attorney, co-chairman in 1964 of California Citizens for Goldwater-Miller.

(d) Dr. Nolan Frizzelle, optometrist, 1964 president of the California Republican Assembly, one of the two important political organizations in the state which operates outside the regular party.

(e) Bruce Reagan (no relation), business executive, a founder of the United Republicans of California, the other state-wide political organization outside the GOP.

(f) Walter Knott, one of the top conservatives and fund-raisers in California.

(g) Henry Salvatori, one of the GOP's chief financial supporters and a strong Nixon and Goldwater backer.

(h) Mrs. Norman Taurog, civic and social leader, a Rockefeller delegate in 1964.

THE *ONLY* CANDIDATE

(i) Jack L. Warner, film executive and a prominent Kuchel supporter.*

Friends of Ronald Reagan went to work lining up other prominent Republicans of every philosophical bent—and raising money as well. By late summer of 1965 a GOP consensus was beginning to coalesce that Ronald Reagan ought to be the man to run against Governor Edmund (Pat) Brown.

The actor surprised a lot of people by displaying more than a passing knowledge of state issues. It was no accident. Spencer and Roberts closeted him with experts on every imaginable California subject, from redwoods to water to taxes to agriculture. Many of them were academicians (especially from UCLA—University of California at Los Angeles) who gave both sides of a problem and recommended books and pamphlets for additional study. Comments Roberts: "Reagan has an extremely retentive mind and is a voracious reader."

By September, Ronald Reagan had pretty much made up his mind to run for the nomination, expressing his growing confidence by publicly saying:

"My initial explorations and conversations lead me to feel that I can obtain the necessary support within my party as well as gain the support of hundreds of thousands of disenchanted Democrats so necessary for a Republican victory."

Democrats had much about which to be disen-

* Warner's enlistment took much of the bite out of the oft-quoted story of what he was reported to have said when told that Reagan might run for governor. "No," said Warner. "Jimmy Stewart for governor. Ronald Reagan for best friend."

chanted and discouraged. No matter where they looked, they were confronted with most unpleasant statistics.

Taxes were up. Per capita state taxes since 1959 (Brown's first year in office) had increased from $117.58 to $157.36. Brown estimated that more than $250 million in new taxes would be needed in 1966.

State spending was up. Brown had proposed a budget of $4.5 billion—the highest state budget ever recorded in U. S. history (until Reagan's first budget). During Brown's tenure in office, California population increased 27 per cent while the state budget increased 87 per cent.

Crime was up, California's crime rate rising 12 per cent in 1965. With nine per cent of the nation's population, California accounted for 17 per cent of the crime.

Prices were up. Pollution and traffic were up. Welfare costs had increased 73 per cent during Brown's administration.

The Berkeley demonstrations and the Watts riots had stained California's reputation from coast to coast.

Governor Brown, though perhaps not responsible for *all* California's problems, had to assume responsibility for them as chief executive—and accept the voters' displeasure as well.

Issues were one side of the frayed Brown image. The other side was the man himself. When asked what he thought of Brown, the average Californian would usually reply, "Well, I like him—but he's kind of indecisive (or bumbling) (or erratic) (or slow) (or naive)."

Democratic leaders could read the writing on

THE *ONLY* CANDIDATE 91

the wall as well as anyone but they were stymied. Brown announced he was going to run for a third four-year term. He had the patronage and the organizational leverage as governor. Furthermore, President Johnson had quietly indicated that Brown was his man and he wanted no fuss and no primary challenge. LBJ was not to get his wish because of the feisty, maverick Democratic mayor of Los Angeles, Sam Yorty.

However, it wasn't all smooth riding for the Reagan bandwagon. In August, a director of the California Republican Assembly declared that Ronald Reagan had boasted that the public relations director of the John Birch Society would endorse him for governor or attack him, whichever would do the most good. If true, the charge would have been damaging in two ways: first, it would have suggested that Reagan was on intimate terms with a top Birch official, lending credence to the claim that he was a "captive" of the extremists; and second, it would have revealed Reagan as a slick political operator and opportunist, rather than the citizen candidate he asserted himself to be.

The CRA director was Mrs. Jane Alexander, who turned out to be a supporter of Joseph Shell for the gubernatorial nomination and, by her own admission, "no fan" of Reagan's. Furthermore, Rousselot had called political manager Bill Roberts months before and had merely offered to "talk up" Reagan in private conversations. Finally, Reagan explained that he had made the reference to Rousselot in a humorous vein but apparently some people had taken him all too seriously.*

* That fall, on October 16, Mrs. Alexander was ousted as a

The Rousselot offer of support was to be a minor irritant to Reagan for the rest of 1965 and throughout 1966. It was one of the major reasons for his statement on the John Birch Society which he released at the annual meeting of the Republican State Central Committee in San Francisco in late September.

By this time, the only Republican who had publicly declared his candidacy for the gubernatorial nomination was Laughlin Waters, a Los Angeles attorney and a former U. S. attorney for Southern California. He was not a significant candidate.

Other possible candidates were former Governor Goodwin Knight, almost 70; conservative Joseph Shell; and the most serious challenger of them all, George Christopher, San Francisco's mayor from 1956 to 1964.*

Christopher was a bona fide liberal who had served as Northern California chairman of Rockefeller's unsuccessful primary drive in 1964. In 1958, he was beaten in the Republican primary for the U. S. Senate nomination by then Governor Knight. In 1962, he was defeated for lieutenant governor by Glenn Anderson although he did come closer to winning than Richard Nixon. Christopher, in the words of one reporter, "looks and talks like a losing television wrestler."

At the September State Central Committee

---

director-at-large of the California Republican Assembly by a vote of 27-9. She was removed on charges that she had embarrassed the CRA by a "breach of confidence" that "brought discredit" on Ronald Reagan.

* Senator Thomas Kuchel, who led every other Republican against Pat Brown in the polls, took himself irrevocably out of the governor's race in mid-September.

meeting, Christopher held a news conference which underscored the reporter's description. One sample of his malaprop prose:

'We (Republicans) have straddled the fence with both ears to the ground at the same time too long."

Christopher also denounced John Birchers—implying that Reagan was their candidate—and the next moment claimed Reagan was once a member of three Communist-front organizations.

Asked to identify the three Communist fronts, Christopher said: "They're in his book." (An apparent reference to Reagan's autobiography, *Where's the Rest of Me?*). Pressed further about his charge, Christopher said he didn't have the names of the three organizations "at my fingertips."

The news conference broke up with reporters shaking their heads and Christopher supporters concealing their despair as best as they could.

At this same meeting, on September 24, 1965, Reagan released a one page statement about the John Birch Society, which became one of his most widely distributed pieces of campaign literature. It deserves to be quoted in its entirety:

"Many words have been spoken and written about the John Birch Society as an issue, particularly with regard to the stance and attitude of the Republican Party, even though the Society claims it is non-partisan and that its membership is almost equally divided between Democrats and Republicans. In recent months my name has been repeatedly injected into articles and discussions concerning the John Birch Society and its membership.

"I have never been and I am not now a member

of the John Birch Society, nor do I have any intention of ever becoming a member. I have never sought Birch Society support, nor do I have any intention of doing so should I become a candidate for public office.

"In my opinion those persons who are members of the John Birch Society have a decision to make concerning the reckless and imprudent statements of their leader, Mr. Welch.

"In all fairness to the members of this Society, I believe this statement would be incomplete if I failed to point out that despite the heavy criticism of the Society by many citizens, Mr. J. Edgar Hoover, Director of the FBI, is on record as stating that the FBI has not investigated the Birch Society because it only investigates subversive organizations. Furthermore, the California Senate Sub-Committee in its 1963 report found the 'Birch Society to be a Right, anti-communist, fundamentalist organization . . . neither secret nor fascist, nor have we found the great majority of its members in California to be mentally unstable, crackpots, or hysterical about the threat of Communist subversion.' The report, however, was highly critical of the Society's domination by its founder, Robert Welch, and of his book, *The Politician,* published several years before the Society was formed. I wish at this time to reaffirm my criticism of Mr. Welch and restate that I am in great disagreement with much of what he says. In my opinion, his charges against former President Eisenhower are utterly reprehensible.

"The 1965 California Senate report does not disavow any of the 1963 findings, but is more critical of the Society mainly because of 'inexcusable actions of a minority of irresponsible members and evidence of anti-semitism in that minority.' According to this report, the Society has grown tremendously since 1963 and has attracted a 'lunatic fringe of emotionally unstable people.' Again, however, the Committee points out they are not representative of the Society's official policy. In my opinion, the Society has a responsibility to maintain vigilance to see that this element does not use the Society for witch-hunting, anti-semitism or any other un-American activity.

"For the record, I would like also to state that I am opposed in principle to seeking support of any blocks or groups because in principle to do so implies a willingness to make promises in return for such support. It would be my intention, if I seek public office, to seek the support of individuals by persuading them to accept my philosophy, not by my accepting theirs. I would campaign on such important issues as the bureaucratic growth of our State Government, the excessive taxation that is already slowing California's economic growth and reducing job opportunities, and the increasing crime rate that makes our cities' streets a place of danger after dark."

Reagan made it clear: he would not seek support of the Society (which does not endorse political candidates anyway); he described Robert Welch as "reckless and imprudent," and he quoted two California legislative reports which criticized the Society but did not make any blanket condemnation of the society. It was to be his firm stand throughout the campaign. As he was to say again and again:

"If anyone chooses to vote for me, they are buying my views, I am not buying theirs."

Still another statement at the meeting, this one by a non-candidate, was to play a major role, not only in the nomination race but in the general election as well. Dr. Gaylord Parkinson, chairman of the California Republican Party, issued a statement to the news media entitled, "Parkinson's Eleventh Commandment." It began:

"I want to tell you how the Republicans are going to conduct themselves in this campaign. . . . That day has passed when we can permit ourselves to air differences we have in the press or on television. To attack another Republican leader in the public media, that Republican will suffer severe reverses. . . .

"The reverses I refer to involve what might be called a revulsion of that candidate across the board. His ratings will drop drastically in the public opinion polls, his workers will wither away, his financial resources will dry up and he will be rejected at the polls."

Parkinson said he was offering his Eleventh Commandment to all who would become Republican candidates in 1966:

"Thou shall not speak ill of any Republican."

Parkinson, while not detailing how he would enforce it, warned that "if henceforth and until November, 1966, any Republican candidate or leader in California deliberately speaks out against the party or against a fellow Republican that activity will endanger his very position of leadership, his candidacy, and most important, the good of the party."

A number of reporters smiled cynically at Parkinson's ploy, remembering the divisive battles of 1958, 1962 and 1964. What they apparently did not realize was that the very memories of those self-destructive campaigns would make the Eleventh Commandment almost irresistible. Beyond dispute, Parkinson's Commandment was to help cement the GOP for the next 15 months, and to make it virtually impossible for candidates like George Christopher to attack without cause the smiling front-runner, Ronald Reagan. The State Central Committee unanimously endorsed the Eleventh Commandment. Reagan was delighted. He knew he needed a united GOP behind him to win the general election.

Chapter Nine

HAT IN THE RING

In the wake of the State Central Committee meeting, at which the efforts of George Christopher and Goodwin Knight upset even their most partisan supporters, anti-Reagan forces within the GOP began casting about frantically for a candidate. The certain black aftermath of a Reagan victory was described for them by Senator Kuchel who urged Republicans to keep a "fanatical neo-Fascist political cult" from taking over the party. The gentle Senator named no names, of course.

In this emotional atmosphere, still another name was suggested: Robert T. Monagan, Republican leader of the State Assembly. At 45, Monagan had established himself in the legislature as an excellent legislator and was looked on with favor by almost all of the liberals and many conservatives as well. But, and it was a big but, Monagan came from a small town in Northern California, the less populous half of the state; he was not well known to the general public; he had no organization and no visible money. Monagan supporters pushed his name hard for several weeks, and did succeed in getting the Republican legislator mentioned in the state and national press. Columnists Rowland Evans and Robert Novak described Monagan as "highly respected" in the California legislature. But that was just about all. Monagan's candidacy, at best a slim possibility, disappeared completely when George Christopher formally announced on October 26, 1965, that he was running for the Republican nomination.

Speaking in ten cities on a whirlwind schedule, the former mayor of San Francisco declared that he had the administrative and executive experience to be governor unlike some others he could name—like Ronald Reagan. He pointed to the polls which showed he was running 4.9 per cent better than Reagan against Pat Brown. He did not mention that the same polls showed him running 10 per cent *behind* Reagan among Republican voters. Eight months later, on the eve of the June primary, Christopher was 17 points behind Reagan among Republicans.

Some comic relief was injected on November 15 when William P. Patrick, a 35-year-old cosmetics manufacturer who had never before run for public office, announced his candidacy for the Republican nomination for governor of California. Patrick was outwardly serious about his intentions and asserted he had $1.5 million to spend on his campaign. He termed himself a progressive Republican with views more like Senator Kuchel "than anyone else in California politics." If he had been a serious candidate, his entry would have hurt liberal Christopher. But Patrick was never a factor although he did obtain considerable publicity for himself and his cosmetics firm.

Three weeks later, at the first annual convention of the California Republican League, a brand-new liberally oriented volunteer organization, candidate Laughlin Waters got off several blasts at Reagan, who also attended the meeting. In his formal remarks, although he refrained from using names, Waters declared: "We cannot afford to put up a candidate who is a political switch-hitter, or a tyro, or who appeals only to a minority even in our own party."

That just about covered all bases: (1) "political switch-hitter" obviously referred to Reagan's past as a liberal Democrat; (2) "tyro" referred to Reagan's non-experience in public office; and (3) "appeals only to a minority" meant, in Waters' opinion, that Reagan's brand of conservatism was very limited in its appeal.

Waters really warmed up during a panel discussion. When Reagan told a questioner that he was "not at this time" a candidate for governor, Waters accused the actor of "political dishonesty," asserting that he had told a group in October that "he had passed the point of no return in his candidacy."

The former U.S. attorney for Southern California also repeated the old story, attributed to Reagan, that John Rousselot, the public relations director of the John Birch Society, had offered to support or oppose Reagan, "whichever was deemed to be better."

As he was to do throughout 1966, Reagan kept his cool. He explained that he had made the remark about Rousselot "facetiously" and reiterated that he was not soliciting the support of the John Birch Society, was not a member and had "no intention of soliciting their support."

As for the nomination, he stated that while it had to be assumed his answer on a formal declaration of candidacy would be yes, "I've also said, of course, you keep one foot back in case the sky starts to fall."

HAT IN THE RING

It didn't and on Jan. 4, 1966, after traveling 10,000 miles and making 150 speeches, Ronald Reagan announced his candidacy for the Republican nomination for governor in a superbly staged television appearance, news conference and public reception. The 30-minute television program was carried on 16 stations throughout the state—a first in California politics for a gubernatorial candidate. A top Reagan advisor told me they used this technique to prevent any Goldwaterizing of the candidate. The heavy use of television was to be a consistent pattern for the rest of the year: put Ronald Reagan directly before the people and let *them* make up their own minds, without benefit of interpretation by anyone, as to whether he would make a good governor.

The timing of the announcement was carefully planned. A preview of the TV program for the news media was followed by a regular news conference which ended at 5 p.m. The program was aired at 6 p.m., meaning that the public had an unobstructed viewing of Reagan.

In his television talk, the candidate, speaking without notes, stressed such bread and butter issues as property taxes (too high), relief (too many "freeloaders"), rising crime, and too high unemployment. Among his proposed solutions were a tax moratorium on homes owned by elderly citizens, an improved business climate, laws permitting "local ordinances that will restore to the police the flexibility and power in making arrests," and higher pay for state legislators.

As he had for many years, he emphasized the dangerous growth of big government, asking: "Can we possibly believe that anyone can manage our lives better than we can manage them ourselves?"

Reagan intended to base his campaign on the belief that the majority's answer would be "no"—if the people could be convinced that a governor *would* let them govern themselves whenever and wherever possible.

The candidate's presentation over television was described by the New York *Times* as "highly effective—so effective in fact, that he stood a solid chance of winning not only the nomination but also the office."

Equally impressive was his performance before 200 reporters (the largest turnout ever for a purely state political event) at the news conference that followed the preview of his TV talk. They threw everything they could think of at Reagan and he caught every one, with a smile. The candidate answered questions from the stage of a ballroom at the Statler Hilton in downtown Los Angeles. The stage was flanked by six-foot photographs of him and his name was spelled out in glittering silver letters that ran some 20 feet across the wall behind him. Nancy Reagan, in a red, fur-trimmed dress, was by his side.

Almost the first question was about the John Birch Society—would he oppose their support?

"It is my understanding," Reagan replied, "that the Birch Society does not support either candidates or political parties and has stated that its membership is roughly, evenly divided between the two parties."

How would he describe his relations with John Rousselot, the Society's director of public relations?

"Well, I haven't seen him for quite some time. The last time really that I was with him was when he was a Republican Congressman and it was friendly."

Had he ever had any discussion with John Birch officials about his candidacy?

"Never."

Did he believe there were members of the Birch Society in the Republican Party?

"I have issued a statement.* It is available here as to how I feel. I am not going to submit a loyalty oath or test to anybody who decides he wants to vote for me. I don't know how I could do it. If anybody decides he wants to vote for me, he has bought my philosophy; I haven't bought his."

Did he believe there was a place in the Republican Party for Birch Society members?

"I think there is a place in any political party for anyone who feels he can conscientiously support the aims and the goals of that party."

More substantive questions were asked. What about Watts; what could be done about the situation there?

"I think one idea, pattern to be extended and followed is the very fine example that has been set by the Los Angeles Chamber of Commerce which has already enlisted the aid of more than 100 industries and expects to expand that (and) has already found jobs for more than a thousand. . . .

"I think an expansion of this is what I referred to in my statement, an expansion of that idea of improving the business climate and seeking out what inducements you could think of, or incentives, to improve the business climate, including

* See pages 93-95, Chapter VIII.

the possibilities of tax incentives. . . . I think basically with a great many of these problems, their solution lies in more jobs for people."

What about his lack of political background?

"As I have stated, I am not a politician in the sense of ever having held public office. My administrative and executive experience has been what I outlined briefly in my statement—business experience. But I just happen to have a deep-seated belief that it is high time that some of the people from the rank-and-file citizenry should involve themselves in government so that it will be a government of and by, as well as for, the people. And feeling that way, I think I can qualify as a citizen-politician and I don't believe that the country was created by men who were politicians."

What about his past as a Democrat; why and when did he become disenchanted?

"My disenchantment was a growing thing. I wasn't as smart as Al Smith; I didn't do it that early. I have often said that I think that there was as much the Democratic Party leaving me, or the leadership of that party leaving me, as my leaving the party."

Was there any real difference between the Republican approach to problems and the Democratic approach such as the Great Society?

"Yes . . . . I again think I voiced it in my statement that I don't believe the pattern that has been laid down by the present Great Society can at the same time include a free society. And I think what we must have in America is the opportunity for all who are willing to accept opportunity; and, at the same time, compassion and care for all those who, through no fault of their own, are unable to accept it.

"You know the Jewish book, the Talmud, has several steps for helping people: the least desirable, the last resort, is the handout, the dole; the most desirable and the most effective is to help people to help themselves and that, I think, probably typifies the Republican approach."

Was he a right-wing Republican?

"No, and I don't believe any more in hyphenating Republicans than I do in hyphenating Americans. I don't think the labels mean anything any more, and I think if people will listen to my specific views in the months ahead on issues and where I stand, there won't be any need for such labels."

How would his campaign appeal to Democrats as well as Republicans?

"Again, I think the problems that face California cross party lines. I think that the solutions *must* cross party lines and I don't know of anyone who knows any better on the Republican side how Democrats think than I do. I was one for most of my life, and I believe that there are millions of fine, patriotic and sincere Democrats who are as concerned as anyone about fiscal irresponsibility, excessive taxation, the growth of government—and I expect to appeal to them."

Would he accept the challenge from George Christopher to have a television debate?

"I'm not in favor and I don't believe in Republican debating Republican in public. I think we have had too much of that already. My contest is with the present administration in Sacramento and I intend to keep it that way."

Would he debate Governor Brown?

"There is a long way until you get to that. There's a primary contest in between. Then I have a hunch that I'll be debating him quite actively in the months ahead. But I don't know. Maybe Mr. Salinger would advise him not to." *

Did he really feel that he could bring about the changes he thought were so necessary in only four years as governor?

"Let me say that anyone would be naive as far as this is, to think that suddenly you could wave a wand and make a great change. I think what has to happen is you first dig in your heels and slow down the toboggan and hope you can bring it to a stop and then you start trying to push it back up the hill. I would think your aim would be, and mine certainly would be, to start pushing it back up the hill as fast as I could. But in the meantime, I'd first be trying to slow it down."

What was the one issue above all others in the campaign?

"To retire Pat Brown."

The reporters roared with laughter, but Pat Brown didn't. He immediately issued a 12-page statement which, the Governor claimed, refuted Reagan's criticisms of him and his administration. It received scant attention. In truth, the Democrats were very worried. The State Democratic chairman, Robert L. Coate, declared that Reagan was "an extremely strong candidate. We fear him." Reagan's Republican opponents were no less concerned.

Sniffed George Christopher about the TV talk: "It was a well-rehearsed production." But he wondered how Reagan would handle such "real-life" problems as crime or tax reform that were outside his world of "make-believe."

* Pierre Salinger was decisively bested by George Murphy in a series of TV debates in 1964.

Laughlin Waters huffed: "I'm all for on-the-job training but not at the gubernatorial level." He added that Reagan's announcement would give the California GOP an opportunity to decide whether it chooses "to attempt again positions which were overwhelmingly rejected nationally and in California during the last election or whether it will return to the moderate and winning position."

Reagan's response to his fellow Republicans was simple and effective: "I will have no word of criticism for any Republican."

The definitive word about his kick-off news conference was written by Carl Greenburg, political editor of the Los Angeles *Times,* and one of the most objective of all California political analysts:

"If Ronald Reagan is the complete political nincompoop his opponents claim, they certainly went to a lot of trouble paying attention to him when he announced his candidacy for the Republican gubernatorial nomination.

"He was drenched in vitriol and sprayed with verbal napalm. . . .

"Whether I agreed with everything Reagan had to say is unimportant, but to this observer his handling of questions at the press conference that followed his announcement indicated Reagan is no novice or babe-in-the-woods."

Chapter Ten

ON THE HUSTINGS

The polls showed that the people liked the actor turned candidate. The State Poll, sponsored by the Los Angeles *Times*, gave Ronald Reagan 41.2 per cent of the Republican vote; George Christopher 27.8 per cent, and former Governor Goodwin J. Knight 9.6 per cent. However, in a sampling of both parties Reagan ranked over Pat Brown by only 46.8 per cent to 42.4 per cent, while George Christopher was far ahead of the Democratic governor, 50.3 per cent to 35.2 per cent. "Goody" Knight also topped Brown by 45.3 to 40.1 The message was clear: Republicans preferred Reagan by a wide margin but the general public wasn't quite sure just what kind of a governor he would make. The brand new candidate set out to convince the people of California that he would do very well indeed.

Campaigning was neither strange nor new to Ronald Reagan. He had campaigned extensively for two presidential candidates and one gubernatorial candidate. In 1953, he campaigned vigorously for Mayor Fletcher Bowron of Los Angeles in a hard fought re-election contest. Nine years later he was honorary campaign chairman for Loyd Wright in his try for the GOP nomination for U.S. Senator.

In his eight years with the *General Electric Theater*, he had traveled tens of thousands of miles back and forth across the United States visiting with and listening to people. Reagan liked to talk, he liked to get up on a platform, he liked the challenge of the question and answer period which follows many speeches. He also happened to believe that the kind of government he proposed was urgently needed. His campaign for better, more responsive, less costly and more creative government swept away many of the public's hesitations and doubts in the next ten months.

He worked hard. He had to. California is not only the largest state in population but the third largest in area, with 156,573 square miles. It has fifty-eight counties, ranging from tiny Alpine with only 400 inhabitants to gigantic, sprawling Los Angeles with seven million people.

California is a state of contrasts and extremes. Its highest point is Mount Whitney, 14,495 feet high. Its lowest point is Death Valley, 282 feet below sea level, the lowest in the nation. It is the nation's leading state in farm marketing income and second only to New York in manufacturing. It ranks first in chickens and turkeys, third in sheep, fifth in cattle. It grows more fruit than you can shake a bowl at. Its vineyards are a major industry in themselves, and produce wines which are as good as anything found in France outside the great Bordeaux and Burgundy growths.

California has Disneyland, Knott's Berry Farm, Balboa Park, Sea World, the San Diego Zoo, three major league baseball teams, four major league football teams, Hollywood, Lake Tahoe, San Simeon, Monterey, the Golden Gate Bridge, and more automobiles than any other state.

California has 182 institutions of higher learning—84 privately owned colleges and universities, 18 state colleges and the famous University of California with its nine-campus complex.

It has sun, sand, surf and snow. It gave birth to the topless dancer, the topless waitress and the topless political worker.*

It has a restless, non-party oriented, TV-minded electorate of eight million men and women who like to confound the pollsters, and often do. It was for their attention and their votes that the candidates vied.

Throughout January and February, Ronald Reagan toured up and down the state in a bus, concentrating his attention and his attacks on Governor Brown and his administration in Sacramento.

He pledged a "moral crusade" to end the "arrogance" of the Brown administration in Sacramento. He spoke of the need for "common sense government." Increasingly he referred to what he called the "creative society," ** which would call upon the talents and abilities of individual citizens, outside as well as inside government, to solve the social and economic problems of California. His favorite target was Pat Brown's $4.6 billion budget, the largest ever submitted to a state legislature.

* In July, 1964, at the GOP National Convention, a young lady in short shorts and a tight blouse selected the partisan-packed lobby of the Mark Hopkins Hotel, headquarters for Barry Goldwater and William Scranton, to remove her blouse and reveal a well-developed unfettered torso while television cameras whirred and whirled.

** A concept suggested by Rev. W. S. McBirnie, pastor of the United Community Church of Glendale and news analyst on a conservative radio program, "Voice of Americanism."

In a televised speech in San Diego in February, Reagan handled the subject in a characteristically visual way:

"Now I've been told that it's politically unwise to talk about (the budget), that for average citizens like us, four billion, six hundred thousand dollars as a figure is meaningless. Well it is, it's incomprehensible. So, I've been trying to get it down to pocket size, because that's where it is going to come from . . . .

"If I have here a four inch stack of thousand dollar bills in my hand, I would be a millionaire. That's a million dollars—that little handful. But if we had that budget piled up in front of us in thousand dollar bills, the pile would be more than one thousand five hundred feet high. . . .

"If you're an average family in California of four, your share of the ante in that budget is a little over a thousand dollars this year. Now I'm just foolish enough to think that the average Californian has some interest in what someone in Sacramento is going to do with his thousand dollars."

By now, the average Californian was listening closely as the candidate told him how Governor Brown and his administration intended to spend his money with a budget "characterized by sloppiness, incompetency and a tendency to sell out the future—our future."

The candidate freely admitted that he was not a fiscal expert but had turned to "the most competent authority I could find on this budget—a man employed by the state to analyze the budget." That is how Alan A. Post, a legislative analyst for fifteen years, became one of Reagan's most quoted authorities during 1966. He used Post's findings again and again to buttress his conclusions of "sloppiness and incompetency" while the Democrats writhed.

As an alternative, candidate Reagan suggested that "instead of harassing business and industry with regressive taxes, let's adopt a creative approach and ask how we can use government to further free the people to allow us to reach our fullest potential. *We have a leadership gap in Sacramento.* They abdicated their responsibility and they continue to seek the answer to every California problem in Washington."

Reagan hit hard at the political machinations of the Brown machine and the inevitable malpractices which mar an administration too long in office. His voice took on a lyrical note as he described his dream of a Reagan administration:

"Picture, if you will, an administration in our state capital without any printed charts listing the minimum campaign contributions that will be acceptable from the state employees. Picture instead an administration that proclaims there will be no solicitation of campaign funds from state employees in any campaign, an administration not characterized by political hacks or hangers on, but one that will seek men to match our mountains.

"That will challenge the men and women of this state to give their time and talents in service to their state and to their fellow citizens and be proud to do so. Out of this great pool of technical skill and talents that is the body politic of California, there isn't any problem that we can't solve if we will refer it to the people and trust the people to find the answer.

"President Eisenhower asked, 'Does political experience automatically result in the creation of a statesman or does it just provide a backlog of men skilled in political give and take?' Well, politically experienced men drew up this budget with very little give—and a great deal of take. Now I'm not a politician and that's precisely why I ask your support, precisely why I'm doing what I'm doing in this point of time. I believe very deeply that the time has come for ordinary citizens to bring honor and morality and the clean fresh air of common sense to government."

It made sense. It had appeal. The average Californian was impressed, and said to his wife, "You know, this guy Reagan sounds like he might make a pretty good governor." The word began to get around, galvanizing his opponents into desperate action.

In late January, the anti-Reagan forces in the Republican Party finally persuaded Laughlin Waters to withdraw from the gubernatorial race and former Governor Goodwin Knight not to enter. This narrowed the field to two major candidates, Reagan and George Christopher, prompting Lawrence E. Davies, the New York *Times* correspondent in San Francisco, to write:

"This means, in the eyes of many observers, a contest of two philosophies—a battle between Ronald Reagan, the actor, with heavy conservative and right-wing support, and former mayor George Christopher of San Francisco, generally pictured as a moderate.

"A straight fight between these two men, Christopher adherents contend, will enable the former Mayor to pin the right-wing label on Mr. Reagan and win the nomination at the June 7 primary.

"Reagan advisers call this stand ridiculous."

It was. Reagan had declared himself a candidate

only after he had satisfied himself that he was acceptable to people in all wings of the GOP. He consistently refused to describe himself as a conservative, right-wing or Goldwater Republican. He shunned labels and hyphens. His initial campaign organization had liberals and conservatives, Rockefeller as well as Goldwater backers from the 1964 primary. The Christopher camp's logic was not compelling but the former mayor and his associates were obliged to try every possible ploy to warn and frighten the party about Reagan.

The Democrats helped as best they could, knowing that Reagan would be the tougher opponent (although they publicly pretended that Christopher was the man they feared). In late January, just a few days before Pat Brown announced for re-election, a statement by all Democratic county chairmen declared:

"Your probable opponent represents a philosophy so divergent from the mainstream of American democratic institutions as to make it imperative that we oppose him with our most able advocate, our best campaigner."

On Feb. 15, Christopher received a boost when Senator Thomas H. Kuchel, the GOP's top office holder who had won re-election by 727,644 votes in 1962, announced his support for the former mayor, calling him the leading "moderate" in the contest for the gubernatorial nomination. At a news conference in Los Angeles, Senator Kuchel said that California needed a governor who would "inspire confidence in people, be unswervingly committed to law and order, believe in equal justice for all and be completely free of the taint of bigotry and hate."

In making the endorsement, the Senator described Christopher as "one who represents Republicans in the Lincoln tradition and the Eisenhower tradition. He is specific and speaks out boldly." Senator Kuchel delivered his endorsement with a straight face. An ideologue, he apparently believed that Reagan was a willing captive of the right wing.

The very next day, the California (Field) Poll reported the following surprising figures:

Among Republicans:
Reagan 38%
Christopher 35%
Undecided 27%

Among Republicans and Democrats:

Christopher	45%	Reagan	40%
Pat Brown	37%	Pat Brown	44%
Undecided	18%	Undecided	16%

This represented a gain of seven points by Christopher against front-runner Reagan among Republicans since the last poll and a similar seven per cent increase by the former mayor over the actor in trial heats against Governor Brown. However, this poll was received with considerable skepticism by many officials in both parties. The skepticism was confirmed within two weeks when the New York *Times'* political correspondent, David Broder, wrote, "At least one private survey taken since the poll appeared Feb. 16 has indicated a 10 point advantage for Mr. Reagan" over Christopher.

George Christopher enjoyed another little surge in his campaign following his Feb. 27 appearance before the Republican State Committee at Coronado, across the bay from San Diego. There, he matched oratorical skill with Ronald Reagan, surprising the 275 members of the committee in attendance. But as the New York *Times* reported:

"Mr. Christopher's stand-off with the actor in the applause rating on his speech failed to shake the view among Republican professionals that Mr. Reagan is the favorite in the primary. . . ."

Christopher's "victory" was easily explained: Reagan had a 102-degree temperature and a case of flu which kept him in bed during most of the weekend meeting. When he took his turn on the rostrum his face was flushed and his voice lacked its usual vibrancy. Christopher rightly took full advantage of his opponent's condition and seized the day.

Reagan was still not up to physical par one week later, on March 6, when he blew up publicly for the first and only time during the campaign. (He was still recovering from an 11-day bout of flu and dysentery.) The setting was the National Negro Republican Assembly's California Convention in Santa Monica. There was an audience of more than one hundred. Reagan, Christopher and William Patrick were invited to present themselves and their views. In his presentation, Reagan said that while he agreed with the goals of the Civil Rights Act, it "was a bad piece of legislation" and that he probably would not have voted for it if he had been in Congress.

In their remarks, both Christopher and Patrick made subtle references to Reagan's statement, playing to the all-Negro audience. Reagan became visibly more tense as the meeting progressed.

In the question and answer period toward the very end, a delegate said, "It grieves me when a leading Republican candidate says the Civil Rights Act is a bad piece of legislation."

At this, Reagan jumped to his feet, threw down some note cards and said loudly:

"I resent the implication that there is any bigotry in my nature. Don't anyone ever imply I lack integrity. I will not stand silent and let anyone imply that—in this or any other group."

In the ensuing hush, he stalked out of the convention hall.

It was just the kind of emotional outburst that an actor and alleged right-winger should never engage in. A Reagan man was quoted as saying: "A couple more like that and it's curtains."

There were no more "like that." Christopher, and Pat Brown after him, tried relentlessly to provoke a similar blow-up but to no avail. The combination of circumstances which had produced the walk-out never occurred again and the Reagan campaign swept on and up, leaving opponents waiting futilely for the candidate to err.

Reagan's explanation of the incident was straightforward. He had been stewing over insinuations by Christopher and Patrick that he was anti-Negro. "Bigotry," he said, "is something I feel so strongly about that I get a lump in my throat when I'm accused falsely."

Chapter Eleven

THE CREATIVE SOCIETY

On March 15, the Watts area of Los Angeles tragically erupted again, resulting in two deaths, about 20 injuries and 49 arrests. Incredibly enough, in the face of the massive 1965 Watts riots when 35 were killed and 1,000 injured, Governor Brown was out of the state and the country when the latest outbreak occurred—although he had been informed of impending trouble by a Negro assemblyman.

Reagan denounced Brown for "flagrant dereliction of duty" by going on a trip to Greece after he had been told about a possible outbreak. He declared that the Governor should have informed Mayor Sam Yorty and Police Chief William Parker of Los Angeles.

Brown replied, rather lamely, that the warning was one of 20 to 25 he had received, that it had not been specific as to time or type of incident and that he *had*, albeit routinely, informed the National Guard.

Mayor Yorty, a just-announced candidate for the Democratic nomination for governor against Brown, stated that Governor Brown had failed to tell him of the Watts rumor.

Reagan and Yorty continued to press Brown hard on this issue for the next three months.

Yorty's entrance into the Democratic primary, although dismissed as inconsequential at first, was to become increasingly significant. If nothing else, Yorty provided Reagan with some quotable language as the Democratic mayor accused the Democratic governor of "indecisiveness and monumental incompetence." Brown, in turn, called Yorty "a cruel, cruel man" and "a renegade."* At this point, Yorty trailed Brown among Democrats by 27.6% to 49.2% but the large number of undecided (23.2%) offered the scrappy mayor an inviting target for his anti-Brown vituperation.

There were other developments:

(1) At the annual convention of the ultra-liberal California Democratic Council, the largest of the party's unofficial organizations, Governor Brown was booed when he defended President Johnson's Vietnam policy. In fact, when he continued to praise the President about 100 of the convention's 1,800 delegates walked out of the hall.

(2) When Jesse Unruh, Speaker of the California Assembly and the state's most powerful Democrat outside of the governor, was asked by a reporter how Brown was getting along, he replied: "Compared to who?"

(3) A Negro newspaper publisher and physician, Dr. Carlton B. Goodlett, filed for the Democratic nomination for governor, declaring:

"The Brown administration came into power in 1958 on a progressive and forward-looking Democratic program. During the ensuing years, Brown has given Californians an increasingly con-

---

* Yorty also said: "The Democratic voters deserve an alternative to the mercenary, corrupt, left-wing, entrenched Brown machine."

servative and, in most instances, an undistinguished state administration. Brown has been a stumbling, gregarious and uninspiring Governor, who lacks both creative initiative as well as the will to put executive drive behind his legislative programs."

April is the month of conventions in California and it was the cruelest month for the fading aspirations of George Christopher. Republican liberals tried hard to counteract the certain endorsement of Reagan by both the California Republican Assembly and the United Republicans of California, the party's two largest unofficial groups. In late March the Republican Council of California endorsed Christopher. The Council was made up of a handful of liberal legislators and party leaders. Its announcement got one paragraph in the New York *Times*.

Two weeks later, the liberal California Republican League, one year old, about 4,000 members strong, endorsed Christopher for governor after having denied Reagan permission to address the delegates at a morning session. The GOP front-runner had asked that the time of his appearance be shifted because a three-day campaign tour had been scheduled before the League had announced its candidates' session. The CRL's president, William P. Gray, turned down the request, but added graciously that he would be happy to acknowledge Reagan's presence.

However, Gray was careful not to allow Reagan's name to be placed in nomination, apparently because he had not addressed the convention. Not one CRL delegate raised his voice in protest, revealing a great deal about the liberal mentality and fondness for fair play.

Following the overwhelming vote for Christopher, William Patrick, the only rival permitted entry, held a news conference at which he angrily charged that the meeting had been "rigged" in favor of the winner. The charge was denied by Gray and Christopher.

And then it was Ronald Reagan's turn. The California Republican Assembly, with 11,500 members, and the United Republicans of California, with 7,500 members, both gave the actor ringing endorsements as their candidate for governor. The CRA, founded 30 years before, had gone conservative in 1964 after several decades of liberal leadership. UROC was founded before the 1964 campaign by a group of conservatives dissatisfied with CRA's liberal ways. Reagan received a hero's welcome at both conventions as he assailed the Brown administration. Christopher, in contrast, continued to make the same basic mistake by ripping into the radical right and candidates who refused to repudiate the radical right—an obvious swipe at Reagan. Christopher was jeered at the CRA convention, which was inexcusable. But the important point is that Christopher never comprehended that the great majority of Republicans were weary of attacks on other Republicans. When Christopher persisted in stomping Reagan rather than Brown, he sealed his fate and his defeat.

Two major issues emerged in May and were quickly picked up by an alert Reagan and his campaign team. In a 153-page report, the State Senate Subcommittee on Un-American Activities accused Clark Kerr, president of the University of California, of having permitted the infiltration of

Communists which had led to "left wing domination" of the Berkeley campus.

The committee's major charges:

(1) President Kerr had allowed Communist-oriented students and non-students to use campus facilities and become the nation-wide "focal point" of the anti-Vietnam war movement.

(2) Under President Kerr, the "campus sank to a new low" morally. Cited in the report were lewd dances featuring "debased spectacles" and promiscuity, widespread intoxication and use of marijuana.

The Committee accused Kerr of "unconditional surrender" of leadership, adding:

"As the campus became more and more politicized by radical elements, what few rules remained were simply ignored. In the name of free speech, civil liberties and academic freedom, the campus at Berkeley has been harboring radicals who have no connection with the institution, and who are allowed to use the state facilities without paying any fees, and to plot acts of civil disobedience that are illegal by their very definition."

Kerr called the report "inaccurate" and "distorted" and challenged the senators to produce evidence of Communists connected with the Berkeley campus.*

Reagan swiftly called on Governor Brown to take immediate action "to restore the university to its once high standing." He kept up the pressure and

---

* One obvious name was Bettina Aptheker, self-admitted Communist and daughter of the leading Communist theoretician in the United States, Herbert Aptheker. Bettina was a prominent leader in the Free Speech Movement along with Mario Savio and also ran for a campus-wide student office. It's unlikely that Kerr had never heard of her at *some* point.

a week later accused Brown of a "cover-up" in asking the U.C. Board of Regents, which included Kerr, rather than the state legislature, to investigate.

Even before the release of the Senate report, Reagan had been criticizing Brown, ex-officio president of the Board of Regents, for failing to exert leadership and take appropriate steps to correct the black image of Berkeley across the country. Berkeley was to become a prime issue in the fall campaign and the one that elicited the most emotional response.

The second major issue was created when the State Supreme Court, by a 5-2 vote, overturned a state constitutional provision permitting owners of private property to sell or rent their real estate to whomever they wanted, without regard for race, creed, or color. The provision thrown out was the famous Proposition 14, approved in a statewide referendum in 1964 by a margin of 2-1. The proposition had nullified the Rumford Act, prohibiting discrimination in property sales or rentals.

To Ronald Reagan the issue was clear. He approved Proposition 14 because it upheld "the right of a man to dispose of his property or not to dispose of it as he sees fit." The Rumford Act, he said, "by infringement on one of our basic individual rights, sets a precedent which threatens individual liberty."

He had been for Proposition 14 in 1964 before it had passed and he was still for it. In contrast, George Christopher loudly applauded the action of the State Supreme Court. Pat Brown did too, although not so loudly. He was adding up the issues and the votes, and too many of them appeared to be coming to rest in the other fellow's corner.

The Reagan bandwagon was now rolling merrily along. In speech after speech, the candidate stressed his main theme—Sacramento extravagance and high taxes. He frequently extended his attack to blame Governor Brown, as a prominent member of the Board of Regents, for the Berkeley demonstrations instituted by a "minority of malcontents, beatniks and filthy-speech advocates."

Gone was any trace of the tension and strain which had erupted at the March meeting with Negro leaders in Santa Monica. He looked good, somewhere in his early forties unless you got within five feet of him (he was now 55). He sounded good, his resonant baritone never seeming to show any sign of strain. He openly enjoyed what he called the "mashed potato circuit" and even when the temperature soared into the 90's, as the New York *Times* conceded, the candidate, "dapper in a black suit and pearl-gray tie, remained unruffled and unperspiring."

Potshots were occasionally taken. *Newsweek* reported that he wore pancake makeup. In a letter to the editor, Reagan rejoined that he had never worn it offstage or while making a speech, explaining, "You see, when I was younger, I could get along without it. And now it wouldn't help any."

The *Saturday Evening Post* began a long article: " 'Sure, he's drawing the crowds,' snorts one rival candidate for political office. 'So would Jayne Mansfield.' "

But even the veteran liberal columnist Marquis Childs was obliged to report, "Reagan seems likely to win the nomination for governor."

And although his critics often made fun of it, pretending not to understand what he was talking about, one of Reagan's major appeals was his Creative Society, which he formally discussed at the University of Southern California on April 19. To emphasize the importance of his subject, he spoke from a prepared text, one of only two times he did so in the primary.

After admitting that he was not a politician, Reagan asserted, "It's time now for dreamers—but practical dreamers—willing to re-implement the original dream which became this nation—that idea that has never fully been tried before in the world—that you and I have the capacity for self-government—the dignity and the ability and the God-given freedom to make our own decisions, to plan our own lives and to control our own destiny."

He argued that we should not automatically turn to the Federal government because "with every ounce of Federal help we get, we surrender an ounce of personal freedom. The Great Society grows greater every day—greater in cost, greater in inefficiency and greater in waste.

"What is needed," he declared, "is not *more* government, but *better* government, seeking a solution to the problems that will not add to bureaucracy, or unbalance the budget, or further centralize power. Therefore, I proposed a constructive alternative to the Great Society which I have chosen to call a Creative Society."

He asserted that "there is no major problem that cannot be resolved by a vigorous and imaginative state administration willing to utilize the tremendous potential of our people."

He gave the assembled students several specific things that a Reagan administration would try to do:

(1) In the area of crime, give local communities the right to pass ordinances for the "protection of the people." Also, call upon the "best minds in the field of human relations and law and penology" for a study of our penal and parole systems.

(2) Create a joint committee of laymen and members of the Bar Association which would choose a panel of outstanding individuals from which the governor would be obliged to "appoint all judges," taking "judicial appointments once and for all out of politics."

(3) Ask the best brains of the business community what is needed to make California attractive once again to industry—the state had fallen from 6th to 13th in attracting new industry in the last five years.

(4) Persuade business to evolve plans for creating job opportunities and a program of on-the-job training.

(5) Study the welfare program with an eye to reducing red tape and excessive regulations—and come up with a welfare rehabilitation program which would eliminate the dole as a way of life for certain citizens.

He mentioned voluntary programs that were working, among them:

(1) United Student Aid Funds, with 65,000 students on 700 campuses who have borrowed $35 million, all of it underwritten by private citizens with no government participation at all.

(2) The cooperation of the Los Angeles Chamber of Commerce along with a group of Negro

businessmen in Watts who put 5,000 people in that area to work.

(3) A California B'nai B'rith Lodge which adopted a youth probation camp and, through a willingness to listen to the young men, reduced the period of time they must stay in camp by one-third.

San Francisco, he reminded them, when destroyed by fire was rebuilt by Californians "who didn't wait for urban renewal."

What is the Creative Society? He asked and answered himself.

"The Creative Society . . . is simply a return to the people of the privilege of self-government, as well as a pledge for more efficient self-government—citizens of proven ability in their fields, serving where their experience qualifies them, proposing common sense answers for California's problems, reviewing governmental structure itself and bringing it into line with the most advanced, modern business practices."

Looking straight out into the audience, he finished:

"This is a practical dream—it's a dream you can believe in—it's a dream worthy of your generation. Better yet, it's a dream that can come true and all we have to do is want it badly enough."

The students responded enthusiastically, clapping and whistling. But this was to be expected—they were young, idealistic. Young people will always respond to a challenge. But unexpectedly their parents, the older people, *also* responded, asking themselves whether this man Reagan was talking straight and whether this thing he called the Creative Society might get the government off their backs, if only a little bit, might lower their taxes, might make them feel the man in the street did matter, did count, could make a difference in what was going on around him. Was he kidding them, they asked themselves, or was he on the level? They looked and listened and wondered, and recorded their decision on June 7, 1966.

Chapter Twelve

LANDSLIDE I

George Christopher kept insisting that what he needed was a large turnout on Primary Day. The conservatives and the right-wingers, he declared, always showed up at the polls. If enough moderates and others (he never said left-wingers) swelled the number of Republican voters beyond the usual number, he had a fighting chance. Christopher got his wish. There was very heavy voting throughout the long sunny day, but as the sun sank in the Pacific, the former mayor of San Francisco sank into political oblivion. Ronald Reagan won the GOP nomination for governor by better than 2-1, carried 53 out of 58 counties and immediately established himself as a favorite to beat Governor Brown in the fall.

In the Republican primary (30,586 precincts reporting), the official returns were:

Ronald Reagan, 1,417,623
George Christopher, 675,683
Three others, 92,751

In percentages, Reagan received 65% of the Republican vote, Christopher only 31%.

In the Democratic primary, the returns were:

Edmund G. (Pat) Brown, 1,355,262
Samuel W. Yorty, 991,088
Four others, 234,046

In percentages, Brown received 52% of the Democratic vote, Yorty 39%.

Brown's slim margin over Yorty underscored Reagan's amazing showing. In a state where Democrats outnumber Republicans by 3 to 2, Reagan had polled 62,000 more votes than Brown. (There is no crossing over in the California primaries.)

There is an old political formula in the Golden State: to win a general election, a Republican must get 90% of his party's votes plus about 25% of the other party's. Reagan and his advisers took a good look at the almost one million Democrats who had voted for Yorty plus the 234,046 who had voted for four also-rans and broke into broad grins. All they had to do was keep preaching unity among the Republicans (thereby holding on to the George Christopher voters) and go after those one and a quarter million anti-Brown votes to win, but big, in November.

The consensus among the California and national press was that Reagan might very well do just that.

Los Angeles *Times:* "The whole thing spells trouble for Brown in his runoff battle with Reagan."

Time: "The Democrats . . . gave Governor Pat Brown his third-term nomination by a sufficiently meager margin to establish Reagan as an attractive even-money bet in November's general election."

Newsweek: "Out of these surprising margins of victory, observers last week spotted a new tide of conservatism—a deep, unsuspected current that could well carry the Republican movie star into the statehouse at Sacramento and stir up a new Goldwatery wave in the national GOP."

Columnist Doris Fleeson: "The California primaries have sung a song of social and political significance to the state and nation. . . . The primary returns certainly suggest that in California at least an underlying tide of dissatisfaction fed by historical and contemporary events is running against the Democrats."

Columnist William S. White: "The immense victory of Ronald Reagan for the gubernatorial nomination is in Party-power terms nothing less than an earthquake. Win or lose in the fall against the incumbent Democratic Governor, Edmund Brown, Reagan has put his brand deeply upon the GOP in the West."

Columnist John Chamberlain: "So it's Ronald Reagan versus Edmund (Pat) Brown in the big California stakes for governor next fall—and it says right here that Reagan is going to win. . . . In a year and a half of campaigning, which included many dangerous question-and-answer set-tos with critical reporters, Reagan did not make a single important slip."

New York *Times* columnist Arthur Krock: "The primary results in California . . . could . . . be a portent . . . that the voters are weary of the repetitious clichés and of the time-worn faces of those in office."

The media also concluded that Reagan's basic appeal was conservative.

Los Angeles *Times:* "A mood of conservatism swept over California politics and politicians in the major races at last Tuesday's election, according to an analysis of the recent surveys and results by the State Poll. Although there were other factors, this emerged as probably the single most important factor of the election."

Los Angeles *Herald-Examiner:* "Ronald Reagan is considered a conservative. And yet he scored a victory of landslide proportions without having had the experience of a veteran political campaigner."

Chicago *Tribune:* "Reagan's victory should silence further talk that voters have no use for anybody who has been devoted to conservative views on government policies."

David Broder, New York *Times:* "Reagan's sweeping victory . . . has given the national Republican party its sharpest tug to the right in two years and placed continued Democratic control of the state in clear jeopardy."

Pollster Lou Harris reported in *Newsweek* that "California is going conservative." Here are the highlights of Harris' significant poll:

(1) "Six out of every ten Republicans in California are conservative. Reagan won over 90% of this vote in the GOP primary."

(2) "Reagan made his most striking showing in the formerly moderate sections of Los Angeles and its suburbs to the east—in Riverside and San Bernardino counties, which now hold one-fourth of the entire state. . . . The bulk of his gain came from the new communities made up of elderly migrants from the Middle West and the young marrieds."

(3) "In 1928, Al Smith lost for President but brought out the big-city Catholic vote that provided a central pivot for Franklin Roosevelt's new majority in 1932. In 1948, Tom Dewey lost but brought into being new suburban Republican power which largely formed the basis of victory for Dwight Eisenhower in 1952.

"Now conservatives are hoping that when Barry

Goldwater lost in 1964, he crystallized a new right-of-center vote in America. It may be too soon to say that the biggest state, often volatile, is the U.S. trend-setter; yet it is now possible this new conservative bloc could provide Ronald Reagan with victory in California in 1966—and in the nation in 1968 or 1972."

Just how important California elections had become nationally was summarized by the liberal newscaster, Howard K. Smith, in a newspaper column just prior to the June 8 primary.

After a few statistics about the truly phenomenal size and growth of the state ("gross annual output of wealth now surpasses that of 100 sovereign nations . . . state's annual budget is exceeded only by budgets of the US, the USSR, Great Britain, West Germany and France . . ."), Smith made his most telling, and pragmatic point:

"There have been 17 presidential elections in the nation since 1900. In 14 of the 17 a New Yorker has been on one of the presidential tickets, because New York had more votes to be won than any other state. Well, the time has now come when it will be obligatory to have a Californian in every Presidential race for the same reason."

However, Ronald Reagan's thoughts were far removed from Presidential races. He set to work immediately building an effective coalition, stating that he would go after everyone, including "the independents because our cause crosses party lines."

In Washington, D.C., Republican National Chairman Ray Bliss, no ideologue but a politician who loves a winner, said: "The sizable majority by which Ronald Reagan won the gubernatorial nomination can now be blended into a united

Republican drive for a complete victory in California in November. As national chairman, I urge all Republicans to unite behind him for governor...."

Senator George Murphy urged all Republicans to accept the primary results "and work together for a restoration of sound and sensible government in Sacramento." Murphy had watched the primary from the sidelines but campaigned strenuously for Reagan and Finch in the fall despite a serious throat operation.

For once in California politics, people seemed to be listening to reason. In Los Angeles, within one week, the leading financial backers of Reagan and Christopher held a news conference at which they announced they were "completely united" behind Reagan. In attendance (for the liberals) were Thomas A. Pike, former assistant secretary of defense under Eisenhower, and Leonard Firestone, of the tire manufacturing company; and (for the conservatives) Henry Salvatori and A. C. (Cy) Rubel.

Commented Salvatori: "The GOP, seldom united in recent years, has finally come through in one piece."

It was a shining hour for Salvatori and Rubel, who less than 18 months before had told Ronald Reagan in his Pacific Palisades home that he was the *only* Republican who could unite the party behind him and win.

It was revealed at the news conference that George Christopher had spent about $450,000 on his primary campaign, almost as much as Reagan, who spent a little more than $500,000.

From San Francisco, Christopher said that while he would certainly *vote* for his victorious opponent in the fall, his active support would depend upon Reagan's position with regard to Senator Kuchel's re-election bid in 1968. Translated, this meant that Christopher would vigorously back Reagan if Reagan would give him assurances that he would support Kuchel two years hence. Christopher was rightly concerned that GOP conservatives would challenge the very liberal Mr. Kuchel in the Republican primary and he wanted Ronald Reagan, as the new head of the party and champion of the conservatives, to prevent so unfortunate (to him) a happening.

Reagan's answer was unequivocating: No deal. He felt that governors should not take positions in primaries and besides, who could tell *who* the candidates would be in two years?

As a result, Christopher remained silent and still throughout the fall. The former mayor was also smarting from two Drew Pearson columns filled with "scurrilous charges" about him which he claimed had been distributed by Brown and Reagan partisans.

The columns rehashed an ancient story (28 years old) about legal troubles which Christopher's dairy had with the State Bureau of Milk Stabilization. Fuming and furious, Christopher lashed out at Pearson and wrote to California papers who normally carried his column. Pearson sued Christopher for $2.6 million, charging libel and interference with livelihood. Christopher responded with a $6 million countersuit.

Brown admitted that members of his staff had talked with Pearson before the columns were published. But when a police mug shot of Christopher began to circulate through the mails, the Governor expressed his shock and declared that his staff had nothing to do with its distribution. Reagan made similar disavowals. Christopher, who has a short temper and a long memory, obviously used the incident as one more reason *not* to go all out for the man who put him out to political pasture.

In view of Christopher's attitude, it came as no surprise to anyone when Senator Kuchel remained silent as to whether he would or would not endorse Reagan. In fact, however, Kuchel had already told the state chairman, Dr. Gaylord Parkinson, that if Ronald Reagan won the nomination he could not support him.

As important as Kuchel was, the real object of Reagan's and Brown's affection was the little maverick mayor, Sam Yorty—and the nearly one million votes he received.

Swallowing his pride and the many insults the Los Angeles mayor had aimed at him during the primary, Pat Brown said at a post-primary news conference that he would rate Yorty as a moderate. Said the governor pointedly: "I'm holding out an olive branch to every progressive and every moderate in California."

At a news conference held later the same afternoon, Reagan stated, "I think the Yorty people are a target for *our* attention, as evidencing dissatisfaction with the administration."

At his conference, Brown presented a brief preview of the coming campaign by describing Reagan as "the crown prince of the extreme right" and a man who "has taken the mantle of leadership from Mr. Goldwater." He added: "Like Barry Goldwater, he is the spokesman for a harsh philosophy of doom and darkness."

Retorted Reagan, "the governor is about two

years behind. He's still running against Goldwater."

And when told that Brown had asserted that there is a white backlash in California, the Republican nominee for governor declared that he would not want to be the beneficiary of such a vote, and riposted:

"I think what took place yesterday was a *Brown* backlash."

With that, Ronald Reagan was off to lay plans to visit the state's Republican Congressional delegation in Washington, make a speech at the National Press Club in the nation's capital and drop in on a very distinguished senior Republican who resides in Gettysburg, Pa.

Chapter Thirteen

COMMON SENSE AND NONSENSE

The old soldier was asked what advice he had given the youthful-looking nominee for Governor.

"I just told him," replied the former President, "to start hitting, keep hitting and when he gets tired to hit harder."

Was his visitor a Presidential possibility?

"Any Republican," he replied, "who wins a governorship and conducts it efficiently on the basis of the welfare of all the people—you can bet he will become a Presidential possibility."

Did he support his visitor for governor?

"Well, I don't know too much about California, but Mr. Reagan is a man of great integrity and common sense and I know he's a Republican and I'm for all Republicans."

The general added that "the Governor and I—there, I'm calling him the Governor already—agreed that if the Republican Party has any label at all it ought to call itself the common sense party."

The visitor smiled broadly and contentedly because "common sense government" was exactly what he had promised he would bring to California if he were elected governor.

Reporters and photographers dutifully recorded the meeting between Dwight D. Eisenhower, 34th

President of the United States, and Ronald Reagan, the gubernatorial candidate of California's Republican Party.

The Washington *Post* reporter wrote that "the 55-year-old actor, looking younger than the cloud-flecked springtime morning, wore a bright blue suit." He added, quite correctly, that a "picture with General Eisenhower is worth a thousand words in any political campaign."

The meeting had come about at the General's suggestion and the candidate had naturally accepted. In fact, the two men had known each other for many years. They had a 55-minute talk at the General's office at Gettysburg College and then lunch at the Eisenhower farm. It was all very cordial and significant for it canceled out the possibility that Senator Kuchel or any other liberal Republican in California would criticize Reagan. He had received the Eisenhower blessing, and that was that. Ike's endorsement also spelled trouble for Pat Brown and his strategy of pinning the extremist-Birch label on Reagan. After all, how could the Democrats convince the California electorate that Reagan was a Birch captive after he had been endorsed by the man whom JBS leader Robert Welch had said was either "shallowly opportunistic" or "consciously serving the Communist conspiracy."

Following the meeting, some elements of the Eastern press jumped to the conclusion that Reagan was trying to "moderate" his image. All too few bothered to draw the more obvious conclusion that Reagan was employing a shrewd political maneuver which defused two of the bigger bombs his opponents had intended to throw at him in the fall.

The following day, Reagan was the luncheon speaker at the prestigious National Press Club in Washington, D.C., graveyard of many an ambitious politician. Robert Donovan, Washington bureau chief of the Los Angeles *Times*, summed up his appearance:

"Ronald Reagan chided Governor Brown, the Great Society and Berkeley beatniks . . . at one of the largest National Press Club luncheons since the visits of Nikita S. Khrushchev and Fidel Castro.

"Suddenly a full-fledged political celebrity in Washington, the Republican nominee for Governor of California gave a witty, deft, engaging performance in his debut in one of the capital's chief forums."

Ted Lewis, Washington bureau chief of the New York *Daily News*, and a veteran reporter who has viewed hundreds of major candidates in a long and distinguished career, wrote:

"In the personality of Reagan there is exactly the sort of political appeal that kingmakers constantly seek. He is deeply serious about the need for change. He has a happy sense of humor. He is a family man, yet, like John F. Kennedy, drives the teen-agers to crazy leaping and squealing. At least, he did in making the Washington rounds today."

It only needs to be added that there were a lot of blasé, middle-aged politicians anxious to meet and be photographed with Reagan.

Columnist Richard Wilson revealed that the new candidate was of concern to the top Democrat of them all: "Even President Johnson pricked up his ears when Reagan came to town. The day afterward he called in Los Angeles Mayor Sam Yorty, presumably to explain to the conservative former

Democratic Congressman why it would be desirable for him to swallow his distaste and support Brown against Reagan."

Back in California, Reagan began to lay plans for the fall campaign with his three top aids: Bill Roberts, 39-year-old partner of the Spencer-Roberts firm; Phil Battaglia, a young 31-year-old lawyer who had performed so brilliantly during the primary that he was appointed campaign manager for the general election; and Lyn Nofziger, a 41year-old political reporter for the Copley News Service. Roberts was a professional campaign consultant and a Republican with no particular ideology. But he had great confidence in Reagan. He had suggested that both Battaglia and Nofziger be hired.

Battaglia was a lawyer and former head of the Los Angeles Junior Chamber of Commerce. He had worked for Kuchel and Nixon in 1962 but was not active in the bitter Goldwater-Rockefeller primary in 1964. He was absolutely tireless and quickly secured the respect and trust of Ronald Reagan. Nofziger was rotund, balding, addicted to cigars and possessed of one of the sharpest wits in Washington where he had plied his writing trade. He had been offered and turned down countless jobs by various Republican organizations (including the Republican National Committee). He was finally persuaded by Bill Roberts, an old friend, to become press director for the Reagan campaign. A conservative, he became in short order a member of the inner circle around the candidate.

In addition, there were four other men who saw Reagan frequently during the fall whose opinion he respected:

Holmes P. Tuttle, 60, one of the original group

of wealthy Republicans who approached the actor in February, 1965.

Ed Mills, 60, a vice president of Holmes Tuttle Enterprises, who served as Southern California finance chairman. Mills had been active for Goldwater, Nixon and Eisenhower.

Taft Schreiber, 57, vice president of MCA, and agent for Ronald Reagan since 1938. He was vice chairman of the candidate's statewide campaign finance committee.

Neil Reagan, 57, the candidate's brother.

Mills and Schreiber, in particular, worked hard and long for Reagan, raising much of the $3 million which was to be spent in the fall.

The Reagan team patiently put together a unity team of Republicans. Caspar Weinberger, a former state GOP chairman and one of the party's leading liberals, was appointed a member of Reagan's steering committee. Also placed on the steering committee were: Dr. Gaylord Parkinson, the Republican state chairman and author of the famous 11th Commandment; State Senator John F. McCarthy, a former Rockefeller leader and minority leader in the Senate; liberal Robert T. Monagan, minority leader in the Assembly, and U. S. Congressman Glen Lipscomb, chairman of the GOP congressional delegation and a conservative.

Several top Christopher supporters were brought aboard, including Marco Hellman, a noted San Francisco financier, who served as the former mayor's state finance chairman; Josiah P. Knowles, co-chairman of the Christopher campaign; J. Max Moore, one of the defeated candidate's closest personal and political friends; and Assemblyman George W. Milias, a top official in the Christopher drive.

With one notable exception, Senator Thomas Kuchel, Reagan and his inner circle were uniting the GOP behind and with them.

Governor Brown was having considerably less success with his fractious, fratricidal party.

His biggest problem remained Sam Yorty and the almost one million Democrats who voted for him. The governor did everything short of rolling a peanut down Wilshire Boulevard with his nose to please Yorty. They held meetings, conferred over the telephone, got their assistants together.

Enjoying to the fullest his position as the catch of the season, courted by both Brown and Reagan, Yorty declared that he *would* endorse Brown *if* the Governor repudiated (1) the Democratic national committeeman, Eugene Wyman; (2) the State Democratic chairman, Robert Coate; and (3) the ultra-liberal California Democratic Council. Yorty added that Brown would also have to give full support to President Johnson's Vietnam policy, sharply and constantly condemned by the CDC, whose support Brown desperately needed.

Brown sighed and went looking for other prominent Democrats. In early July, he held a news conference with Assembly Speaker Jesse Unruh and Senate President Pro Tem Hugh Burns, both of whom declared their "enthusiastic" support of the governor. Unruh and Brown had been at odds for several years because of the Speaker's political ambitions which the Governor had tried to thwart. Now, faced by the very real possibility of a Republican victory, they ostensibly joined forces, and Brown spoke confidently of a "new ball game."

The bonhommie did not last very long. One month later, on Aug. 13, a sharp fight broke out in Sacramento over the choice of a new Democratic state chairman. The two candidates were Mrs. Carmen Warschaw and Assemblyman Charles Warren. Nicknamed "the Dragon Lady," Mrs. Warschaw was favored by Unruh, Frederick Dutton who was brought in by the governor as his top campaign strategist, and Brown himself. Warren was backed by Don Bradley, Brown's official campaign manager, Lt. Gov. Glenn Anderson and most Democratic clubs.

Warren won by a vote of 447-443. Republicans were quick to make the obvious point that the governor couldn't control his own party.

At this same meeting of the State Democratic Central Committee, Brown shocked many liberals by announcing that he was going to appoint a bipartisan commission of "the state's most outstanding citizens to consider amendments to or a substitute for the Rumford Act," the state's open housing act.

There was some applause, but several delegates shook their heads and later sat silently during a standing ovation.

Remarked a Negro assemblyman from San Francisco, William L. Brown, Jr., "He sounded like Reagan."

It was an obvious and embarrassing retreat for Brown, who had pushed the Rumford Act through the State Legislature in 1963. Brown's expediency was all the more apparent because it followed by one week the Republican state convention at which Reagan, in conformity with his principles, had promised to campaign for repeal and replacement or amendment of the Rumford Act.

The polls held little cheer for the embattled governor. The California Poll, conducted by Mervin Field, reported that Reagan was the favorite of 52%, Brown, 37%, with 11% still undecided. Field said that such an advantage had not been registered by any gubernatorial candidate since Earl Warren 20 years before.

At the Democratic state convention, Brown tried to split the Republicans, referring constantly to Kuchel, Christopher, Nixon and Knight as traditional progressives "with almost nothing in common" with Reagan. Earlier he had traveled to San Francisco to apologize personally to Christopher for the "scurrilous" Drew Pearson columns about the former mayor.

Within one week, Goodwin Knight announced that he had accepted an appointment as chairman of a Republican effort to elect state legislators, adding:

"Electing Ronald Reagan governor without electing a Republican majority in the Legislature would be inexcusable. Since completing my term as governor in 1958, the Republicans have lost control of the state government. Reapportionment gives us a golden opportunity to recapture the Legislature."

As Batman might say, "Zap!"

As for the others, Christopher was locked in because of Ike's endorsement and the unity actions of most of his top supporters. Nixon was not about to pick a fight with Reagan, if for no other reason than its adverse effect on Robert Finch, a friend and advisor, who was running for lieutenant governor on the Reagan ticket. That left only the self-isolated Kuchel, who was to say or do nothing for either candidate in the fall.

In his quest for GOP votes, Brown even hired a campaign management firm which usually handles Republicans—Baus and Ross, which ostensibly handled Barry Goldwater's successful Presidential primary in California in 1964. I say "ostensibly" because I was in California in May, 1964, as one member of the Goldwater team brought in to save a faltering campaign. One of the major reasons why Goldwater was in trouble and why eight of us were flown in from national headquarters in Washington was the unaccountably lack-luster performance and incomplete planning of Baus and Ross. When their appointment to assist Brown was announced, one political observer commented, "Now I *know* Reagan will win."

Something had to be done about good old Pat Brown. The gloom at the state AFL-CIO convention in early August was as thick as Los Angeles smog on a bad day. It was clearly time for extreme measures. Back in June, a Brown advisor had revealed that a team of researchers were scrutinizing Ronald Reagan's career and background. Was a "smear" intended? Replied the advisor:

"The word 'smear' is used rather loosely. I gather every time you analyze a man's character you'll have the word 'smear' thrown at you. In my book the word 'smear' means something that is untrue. I don't think we will hold back on the truth just because it might be called a smear."

What was the truth? Pat Brown had revealed it the day after the primary, referring to his opponent as "the crown prince of the radical right."

The "proof" came in two parts. On July 28, State Controller Alan Cranston released a 26-page report on the John Birch Society, charging that it was "riddled" with anti-Semitism. For four days,

Cranston attempted to deliver personally a copy of his report to Reagan, following the Republican candidate up and down the state, complaining that Reagan was ducking him. At last they met at Los Angeles International Airport. Reagan accepted the report and commented, "You've made your grandstand play. Why don't you go out and campaign against Mr. Flournoy?" (The Republican nominee for state controller.)

After reading the report, Reagan referred reporters to his basic statement on the John Birch Society, in which he stated he would not seek its support, and added, "It's no secret that I deplore racism of any kind."

Democratic State Chairman Robert Coate quickly stated that Reagan's comments and his refusal to debate Cranston showed that the GOP candidate "is an apologist for and is supported by the John Birch Society. . . ." Within the next week, Coate said, Democrats "will complete and make public a profound document proving that Reagan is the willing associate and collaborator of some of the most obnoxious extremist causes in America."

The 29-page "profound document" was released on August 11 by Mr. Coate. It was entitled: "Ronald Reagan, Extremist Collaborator—An Exposé." It charged:

"That he (Reagan) has collaborated directly with a score of top leaders of the super-secret John Birch Society.

"That his campaign organization is riddled with members of the society.

"That he supports the programs, policies and projects of numerous extremist fronts.

"That the extremist money from California and

eastern states is an important source of his campaign financing."

Among the supporting "evidence" were the following facts:

• Reagan had cooperated with Birchers in 1964 to keep the "ultra-right wing magazine," *Human Events,* financially afloat. *Human Events,* a weekly tabloid published in Washington, D.C., is about as ultra-right as *Reader's Digest.*

• Reagan was an advisor of the "extreme right" Young Americans for Freedom. YAF has several hundred distinguished Americans on its senior advisory board, including 43 members of the U. S. House of Representatives and Senate, both Democrats and Republicans.

• Reagan had campaigned for Congressman John Rousselot, a prominent member of the JBS, in 1962 (see page 74 for an explanation of this old bromide.)

• Reagan had appeared in 1961 in support of Dr. Fred Schwarz's "Christian Anti-Communism Crusade." Dr. Schwarz's book, *You Can Trust the Communists (To Be Communists),* is widely recognized as one of the best primers on communism published in the last 20 years.

Listed by Coate as members of what he called "Reagan's Rightist Brain Trust" were Patrick J. Frawley, Jr., president of the Schick Safety Razor Company; Henry Salvatori, Walter Knott, industrialist C. C. Moseley and Loyd Wright.

Reporters pressed Coate about Reagan's extremist connections. No, Coate did not believe that Reagan was a Bircher. No, he did not know of any ranking John Birch Society member who was a day-to-day advisor. No, he did not think that Reagan was bigoted. Yes, it was true that genuine conservatives supported Reagan but "they do not call the shots."

The same day Reagan held an impromptu news conference at the Century Plaza Hotel in Los Angeles where he was meeting with several Jewish business leaders, who did *not* refuse to meet the alleged "extremist collaborator." The GOP candidate said that it was "absolutely not true" that he was under the power or influence of extremist groups. The following day he called the leaflet a "smear" and a tactic used by the Democrats because Governor Brown "does not dare campaign on the issues." He added that he would continue to "repudiate anyone or everyone who is a racist or bigot." Concluded Reagan: "The governor won't run on his record, so he has this phony issue. . . . Come October, they're going to come in dripping mud up to their elbows and say they've never seen such a dirty campaign."

Later, a close Reagan advisor commented: "Our feeling has been we are just not bothering to reply to this type of charge. They are trying to run our campaign for us. We are running against Pat Brown, not anyone else."

Right or wrong? Shrewd psychology or wishful thinking? The newspapers were filled for several days with Coate's charges as were radio and television news programs. The Democrats happily concluded that at last they had an issue and they trundled out the cannon. Pat Brown declared that "Reagan was a handsome, smiling puppet reading the script of the John Birch Society." Lt. Governor Glenn Anderson called Reagan "unstable" and asserted that the Republican candidate had "been for almost every crackpot gimmick, every shallow fraud, every silly novelty that has been proposed."

He said that "Reagan is about as conservative as the leader of a mob of self-appointed vigilantes."

Unruffled, Reagan kept hitting the Brown administration about taxes, spending, Berkeley, the need for morality in government. In short, he refused to panic.* He went right on being the calm, reasonable, persuasive candidate he had been throughout 1966. The people took one look at what the Democrats were saying about Reagan (puppet, unstable, extremist) and then a look at Reagan in person, on television, on a platform, in a parade, and decided that somebody had to be very wrong. As the election returns were to prove, the Democrats overdid it just as Rockefeller's people had back in the spring of 1964 when they kept implying that Barry Goldwater was unstable and an extremist who couldn't be trusted in the same room with an H-bomb (a major Rockefeller mailing piece in California was entitled, "Who Do You Want in the Room With the H-Bomb?").

The Democrats unveiled their big exposé and to their dismay the public yawned.

---

* His standard reply was: "We welcome anyone's inspection of our organization. No member of the John Birch Society will be found." But he also added, typically and fairly, "It never occurred to me to give a saliva test to the people who have supported me."

Chapter Fourteen

"A PRAIRIE FIRE"

Although each man had been campaigning since the first of the year, Ronald Reagan and Pat Brown were expected to observe an old political ritual by officially kicking off their campaigns on Labor Day, September 5. Obedient to custom as usual, the governor went to Los Angeles where he told a Catholic Labor Institute that his administration had a good record against crime. He accused the Republicans of trying "to peddle phony election-year statistics" about crime but openly revealed that all was not right by presenting a detailed anti-crime program of his own. Three of his proposals—tougher anti-pornography laws, more protection for citizens, and state assistance for local crime prevention agencies—echoed earlier Reagan suggestions.

The Los Angeles *Times* later asked editorially: "How much will (these proposals) cost and where will the money come from?

"A cost-conscious electorate is entitled to the answers.

"This is particularly so because on the same day he presented his crime program, Brown pledged to seek a reduction in property taxes. . . .

"Taxpayers should bear in mind that even if

no new programs are instituted by the incoming administration, they still face a whopping tax increase next year—just to pay for expanding programs already underway."

The next day, Governor Brown and Mayor Sam Yorty rode in a downtown parade marking the 185th birthday of Los Angeles. Just one thing marred this touching display of togetherness—the governor and the mayor rode in separate cars. Following the parade, Brown left to make a campaign speech in Ventura while Yorty moved to the reviewing stand whose honored guests included—Ronald Reagan.

By now Pat Brown was beginning to feel like the Ancient Mariner, only he had trouble everywhere. Five days earlier, several disenchanted, disgruntled Democratic liberals (including Edward Keating, then publisher of *Ramparts* magazine) announced they would hold a statewide Conference on Power and Politics Sept. 30 - Oct. 1. The liberals described both Brown and Reagan as "know-nothings" and explained that a defeat of Brown "could reinforce the liberal wing of the Democratic Party." They stated that one of the major speeches at the conference would be made by Julian Bond, public relations director of the mis-named Student Non-Violent Coordinating Committee (SNCC), an invitation not calculated to soothe an already riot-shy state.

However, all was not doom and gloom for the beleaguered Brown. On September 2, the Field Poll reported that the gap between the two candidates had narrowed sharply since the last polling in June, immediately following the primaries. The Field results:

	September	Mid-June
Reagan	46%	52%
Brown	43%	37%
Undecided	11%	11%

A 15% advantage had been trimmed to only 3%. Field stated that Brown had won over a "significant portion" of the Democrats who voted for Mayor Yorty and other Democrats. He also reported that there had been a shift of Republicans who had backed George Christopher to Ronald Reagan.

Although cheerier news than Pat Brown had recently been getting, the poll still showed that in the more populous south Reagan held a sizeable 49 to 42% lead, with 9% undecided. Brown had to cut into that margin or suffer an overwhelming defeat. To do that, he had to spur his Party to greater efforts than ever before. But as Gerald Hill, president of the ultra-liberal California Democratic Council, told a Los Angeles *Times* reporter, "It's true that fewer are sitting on their hands now than a month ago. The spirit is starting to pick up some. But the real damage to Brown is that so far the campaign has not excited the activists, who are the liberals."

Reagan had no difficulty in exciting his supporters on Friday, September 9 (the 116th Anniversary of California's entry into the Union) when he formally launched his campaign in a speech at Los Angeles' Biltmore Bowl. The address was telecast over a statewide network. The hard news in his remarks was his promise that if elected governor he would appoint John McCone, former head of the Central Intelligence Agency, to head a "blue ribbon" commission to conduct a "fair and open" inquiry into University of California affairs.* That got the headlines. But what impressed those watching was the soundness of the Republican candidate's analysis of the state's major problems. He certainly didn't look or sound like an extremist as he asserted that he would (1) retain the state's system of unemployment insurance; (2) strengthen the system of social security by eliminating the earnings limitation on those who wished to augment their pensions and by extending coverage to everyone over 65; (3) continue to oppose right to work laws "as too big a gun for the problems we seek to solve" but would push for a "secret ballot" on all union votes; (4) continue welfare aid to those in need but promised there would be "no pay for play."

The GOP candidate hit hard, although not by name, at Senators Robert Kennedy and Abraham Ribicoff for "insulting" Mayor Sam Yorty at a recent Washington, D.C., hearing through "an arrogant display of bad manners." He added that he hoped Senator Kennedy would come to California on behalf of Pat Brown because "it would be interesting to have this citizen of Massachusetts, who serves as the Senator from New York, explain why he's qualified to tell us how to run the state of California." The audience roared their appreciation.

He also criticized two regents of the University of California, declaring that they violated an obligation "not to get involved in partisan politics." At an ensuing news conference he identified one regent as Frederick Dutton, serving as Brown's campaign manager, and the other as Wil-

* An irreproachable selection: Governor Brown had selected McCone to head an inquiry into the 1965 Watts riots.

liam Coblentz, who is "organizing university professors to help school the governor on the issues."

In that soaring lyrical style which many had come to expect of him, Reagan concluded:

"We can start a prairie fire that will sweep the nation and prove we are number one in more than size and crime and taxes. This is a dream, as big and golden as California itself.

"It's a dream that knows no partisanship. Millions of patriotic Democrats will join us bringing that dream to fulfillment because they, too, believe in a 'Creative Society' mobilizing the full resources of our people, bringing the common sense of the people to bear on all the problems, restoring pride in ourselves, our government and our state and nation.

"We can 'get up astounding enterprises and rush them through with magnificent dash and daring.'

"William Penn said: 'If men be good, government cannot be bad.'

"Our people are good. Our government can be."

Pat Brown retorted that California's government had not only been outstanding but had won national recognition. As proof, he offered the "impartial" testimony of the first of a number of Great Society Democrats who were to visit the Golden State that fall: Interior Secretary Stewart Udall. After praising the conservation policies of California, Udall hinted broadly that if Ronald Reagan were elected governor, the state might not receive as much Federal assistance.

"My department can help, as it is now helping with many of California's water problems," the Secretary of the Interior said. "But the help we can offer, under both existing programs and those yet to come, will continue to be effective *only* in the context of an imaginative, progressive, enlightened program of state leadership and action."

Udall announced that he would be back next week with Mrs. Lyndon Johnson, who would join Governor and Mrs. Brown in dedicating Point Reyes National Seashore and Scenic Highway One. Others scheduled to drop by, Brown aides announced, were Vice President Hubert Humphrey, Senator Robert Kennedy and Agriculture Secretary Orville Freeman, all friends of Pat Brown.

In contrast, Reagan had declared back in June that he planned a campaign with only the help of Californians. "This isn't a case of Senator Goldwater or Nixon or anyone else," he explained. "I believe it's between the candidates and the people. I'm not going to ask any national figure to come in and campaign for us."

The governor's next major ploy was worthy of its setting. Speaking to a joint meeting of judges and lawyers at the state bar convention at the Disneyland Hotel on Sept. 21, he asked that crime, the courts, the Rumford Act *and* the University of California be removed as issues in the campaign. "We need," said Brown, "sanity, clear thinking and an end to irresponsible rabble-rousing from any side."

And an end, as well, to four issues which were bothering the hell out of him, and the voters.

His call for an elimination of the Rumford Act as an issue followed by only six days a Field Poll which reported that 68% of the people favored either repeal or reform of the Act, and appeared on the *same* day as a State Poll which revealed that 72% of the people supported the right of a property owner to discriminate in any way he sees fit with regard to the sale or rental of his property.

To no one's amazement, Reagan declined to stop talking about the major issues of the campaign, which inevitably began to attract the usual procession of national columnists and reporters who made some not-so-usual conclusions.

Liberal columnists Rowland Evans and Robert Novak reported on September 24 that the "Birch issue indeed is dead. . . . Polls taken by both camps showed Californians—particularly the 60 per cent of the state's population that lives in Los Angeles, Orange and San Diego Counties in Southern California—couldn't care less about the John Birch Society or right-wing extremism issue. What bothers them much more is the Negro revolution and high taxes."

Reporter David Broder of the staunchly liberal Washington *Post* wrote on September 18: "There is . . . coming into view—a man who is more old-shoe likable than Hollywood glamorous, more pragmatic than doctrinaire; a man with an open mind, an inquiring intelligence and a healthy ambition.

"His top political advisors believe this Reagan can be elected Governor of California and quite logically, become a strong contender for the 1968 Republican presidential nomination."

George Nobbe of the usually conservative New York *Daily News* wrote on October 2: "He can talk thoroughbred horses with grizzled ranchers, argue college morals with beatnik coeds, greet old movie fans, and put down hecklers with a pleasure that is obvious, all the while signing autographs—and without taking his eyes from the person who is talking to him.

"A sort of homey philosophy is woven into The

Speech from start to finish and, if it sounds a little cornball, that's Ronald Reagan. . . .

"He insists he wrote The Speech himself, though he doesn't say just when, and the more you hear him give it, the more inclined you are to believe him, because it *sounds* like Ronald Reagan."

In the New York *Times* on October 2, Warren Weaver wrote of the "rather startling interpretation" Reagan placed on his lack of experience, quoting the candidate as saying:

"Nowhere in the state constitution does it say to be governor you have to be a professional politician, and I'm not. This country was created by ordinary citizens, not by politicians, to be run by ordinary citizens.

"I think it's time for ordinary citizens like you and me to bring some common sense thinking to all these problems that have been created in California in the past eight years by the professional politicians."

Inevitably, Hollywood got into the act—on both sides. Stars like Frank Sinatra, Joey Bishop, Danny Kaye, Trini Lopez, Dean Martin, Keely Smith, Danny Thomas and Nancy Wilson entertained at Democratic fund-raising events. GOP events were treated to the likes of Walter Brennan, Buddy Ebsen, George Chandler and Andy Devine. In addition, such Democrats as Kirk Douglas, Burt Lancaster, Gene Kelly, Dan Blocker and John Forsythe appeared on television and radio, all uttering variations on this theme: "I could play a governor in a movie, but I don't have the ability to be one." Maybe *you* don't, but Ronald Reagan *does*, argued Republicans Pat Boone, Irene Dunne, Chuck Connors, Ruby Keeler, Fred MacMurray, Roy Rogers, Fess Parker and John Wayne.

Wrote AP film columnist Bob Thomas: "This autumn's outburst of political activity by actors is the greatest ever seen for a State campaign. The reason is both ideological and personal; aside from their political feelings, many actors feel strongly about whether one of their profession is or is not fit for high public office."

One voting bloc, in particular, shuddered at the possibility of a citizen like Ronald Reagan in the governor's mansion—organized labor.

Way back in July, labor columnist Victor Riesel wrote that the AFL-CIO planned to "raise at least $3 million inside labor alone for Brown's supreme conflict." At their state convention in early September, California labor leaders rammed through a special dues increase plus a call for a "voluntary contribution" of $1 per union member to build a $1.5 million war chest. Labor organizers were appointed for every Congressional district. A massive voter registration drive was begun. Labor papers were filled with the full text of the Democratic exposé, "Ronald Reagan, Extremist Collaborator." Although Reagan protested that he was not anti-labor (after all, he had served six terms as president of an AFL union) and that he was *not* for Right to Work laws (he campaigned against them in 1958 when they were a major state issue), union leaders insisted that he was a front man for right-wing extremists who would block future economic and social gains for working people. The word had gone out from AFL-CIO headquarters in Washington: Get Reagan.

The White House concurred. And so Vice President Hubert Humphrey came, he saw, but he conquered very little. In a major speech in Los Angeles he contented himself with describing Pat

Brown as "a big man with a big heart" who is "more than a shadow on any silver screen."

Humphrey instructed aides to strike from his prepared speech two full pages of wisecracks about Reagan, based on his movie roles and brief experience in politics. Some Democrats were beginning to conclude that they had been overemphasizing Reagan in the campaign. Others kept on beating the extremist drum. The disagreement was more evidence of a confused and cantankerous Democratic party split four ways—among the ultra-liberals of the California Democratic Council (CDC), the Brown loyalists, the Unruh "power brokers" and the Yorty insurgents.

Then on September 28 a riot broke out in San Francisco. During the four-hour outburst a 16-year-old Negro boy was killed by a policeman. Governor Brown immediately called out 2000 National Guardsmen, moving swiftly to prevent any charge of negligence similar to that which he suffered during the Watts riot in March when he was touring Greece. Some Democrats said that Brown's acting with such dispatch reassured the voters. But all the stories rehashed the previous riots, including the Watts outbreaks of 1965 and 1966. Three weeks later, on October 19, violence exploded in Oakland, across the Bay from San Francisco. Hundreds of juveniles smashed equipment at schools and grocery stores, assaulted teachers, threw gasoline bombs and called in false alarms. About 30 were arrested. The two racial outbursts jolted the people of northern California, which has traditionally considered itself the more enlightened half of the state.

During a televised joint appearance with the governor, Reagan said that he thought the new disorders were "an indication of a lack of leadership in Sacramento." Brown countered that he thought the riots were the action of an "extremist" minority. Most political observers agreed that they reinforced a growing conviction that it was time for a change in Sacramento.*

The October 11 California Poll, conducted by Mervin Field, confirmed the suspicion:

	Today	September	June
Reagan	46%	46%	52%
Brown	39%	43%	37%
Undecided	15%	11%	11%

Field concluded that "Brown's drive to close the gap on Ronald Reagan has apparently stalled." The governor was seven points down with less than a month to go. Significantly, according to Field, 16% of the Democrats were undecided on how to vote, and a "large majority of the Democrats who voted for Los Angeles Mayor Sam Yorty and others who contested Brown in the primary election are still not giving Brown their support."

The New York *Times* became so agitated that it wrote an unprecedented editorial concluding: "Governor Brown belongs at the State Capitol in Sacramento, dealing with the stubborn public problems he knows so well; Mr. Reagan belongs in the studios in Hollywood, gracing the movie and television screens he knows so well. On Nov. 8, Californians will, we trust, understand where reality ends and fantasy begins."

Ramparts Magazine, another liberal publication, disagreed with the *Times*' definitions, editorially describing Pat Brown as a "lumpfish," who

---

* One of the most effective Reagan slogans, used in Spanish-American areas, was, *"Ya Basta?"* ("Had Enough?")

is "distinguished by his completely undistinguished appearance . . . enjoys mouthing platitudes . . . but his weak backbone keeps him from acting upon them . . . . When not drifting along with the prevailing currents, he enjoys floundering in a sea of expedience."

In contrast to these stormy seas, Reagan was enjoying smooth sailing.

In early October he received a warm endorsement from a formidable vote getter, Dr. Max Rafferty, State Superintendent of Public Instruction, who in June had polled the largest vote ever received by a candidate for non-partisan office in California. His total of three million votes was more than the combined totals for Reagan and Brown. Rafferty sent education questionnaires to both candidates. Brown, well aware of Rafferty's conservative bent, refused to answer. Reagan's replies made it clear that he favored more local control over the schools and intended to meet with the Board of Regents to persuade them to adopt regulations which will prevent "treasonable and immoral conditions" within the university.

All the while, aides to Brown and Reagan had been trying to agree on a proper format for a fullfledged debate between the two candidates. When a debate had first been suggested in early September, Reagan said, "Sure, why not?" To some people's surprise, Brown also accepted. It was one of the governor's shrewdest campaign moves. In a face to face debate with a more eloquent and skilled speaker, Pat Brown had to score well—because he would be expected to be demolished. The situation was similar to 1960 when just about everyone (except Nixon and Kennedy) thought beforehand that Nixon, the man who had stood up to Khrushchev, would crush the less experienced JFK. When Kennedy more than held his own, millions of votes shifted. Brown hoped to pull off the same trick in 1966. But he wanted a little insurance and asked for a news panel format. Reagan preferred a straight debate. The air was filled with charge and counter-charge, accusation and counter-accusation. In the end, there was no debate, although the two men did appear together on three television programs. The consensus? Pat Brown did surprisingly well.

But there was no sign anywhere that he was pulling ahead of the Republican candidate. And it didn't look as though Reagan was going to make a serious mistake—like losing his temper and stalking out of a meeting. Well, they could always *try* to make him mad. Call him names, someone suggested, imply he's a bigot. That seems to get under his skin. Brown obliged.

On October 6, in Los Banos, Brown called Reagan "one of the most dangerous right-wing candidates this country has ever seen."

On October 7, in San Francisco, Brown said that members of the John Birch Society are "the storm troopers" of Ronald Reagan's "drive for governor."

But the governor outdid himself in a special television program that, for undiluted demagoguery, topped the Democrats' TV spots against Barry Goldwater in the 1964 presidential campaign. The 30-minute film was called, "A Man Against the Actor," and was telecast 100 times throughout the state in the final ten days of the campaign. In its most controversial scene, Brown is talking to a group of Negro children.

"You know," he tells them, "I'm running against an actor . . . and you know who it was who shot Abe Lincoln, don't you?"*

All it lacked was a doctored film clip of Ronald Reagan playing John Wilkes Booth. But the Democrats had again misjudged the gullibility of the California electorate. Reagan ordered a poll which showed that the voters were not impressed by so obvious a smear. The results on Nov. 8 proved that the public had reacted against the marksman rather than the target.

Another sample of Democratic subtlety was a leaflet distributed among union groups which shrieked, "The Target Is Your Family." It charged that Reagan favored up to $1,000 a year tuition at state colleges (not true), opposed accepting Federal aid to education (not true), had supported the idea of a voluntary social security system (Reagan was for a voluntary option, not system), and opposed further land acquisition for public recreation (not true).

As he had for ten long months, Ronald Reagan stuck to the issues.

On October 1, in San Diego, Reagan called for tuition at the University of California, warning that the alternative might be a cutback in the entire "higher education program."

On October 9, in San Mateo, he asked Democrats to join with him to restore balance to the two-party system. In a rare reference to the Vietnam war, he said: "Rank and file Democrats don't believe we should stop bombing in North Vietnam when the weapons to fight in South Vietnam are coming from North Vietnam." To Democrats, he

---

* The Democrats made a one-minute TV "spot" of this scene and saturated the state with it in the last week.

"A PRAIRIE FIRE"

said: "There is only one way to get your party back and that is to throw that gang out of Sacramento."

On October 13, in Riverside, Reagan hit hard at Brown's call for a commission to examine the Rumford Act, which he once supported. "This ploy is so obvious," stated Reagan, "that many good people asked to serve on the commission refused and it took him weeks to round up a commission. It's too late and too little." Reagan reiterated his position that a property owner should have the right to sell or rent to whomever he pleased.

On October 23, in Concord, Reagan called for a "yes" vote on Proposition 16 (CLEAN) so "we can have a mandate from the people" on the subject of obscenity. (Proposition 16 was a measure on the ballot which would have redefined what is obscene material and written the new definition into state law. It also would have set up new and tougher procedures for prosecution of those dealing in obscene material. The public favored Proposition 16 by 2-1, according to the State Poll.) Reagan emphasized that as governor he would guard "against any kind of book burning."*

Bobby Kennedy came to California in late October and was greeted by signs saying, "Carpetbagger," "Beware, This Is Yorty Country," "Aren't Two States Enough?" The Senator called Governor Brown, who traveled with him during his two day trip, "an inspiration to the rest of the nation." But he was careful to make no direct attack on Reagan.

Newspapers began to publish their endorsements. The Los Angeles *Herald Examiner* (a

---

* Despite the polls, Proposition 16 was rejected by more than 600,000 votes on election day.

Hearst paper, daily circulation, 724,273) endorsed Pat Brown, saying that "although we have disagreed with Gov. Brown on many occasions, and if he is re-elected there no doubt will be other differences of opinion, we believe the over-all record of his administration warrants his re-election." Smaller papers like the Riverside *Press Enterprise*, the Palo Alto *Times* and the Redwood City *Tribune* also endorsed Pat Brown with but-studded editorials.

But the important endorsement, the Big One, is that of the West Coast's publishing goliath, the Los Angeles *Times* (daily circulation, 812,147, Sunday, 1,149,295), which on Oct. 16 declared:

"The *Times* earnestly believes that the election of Ronald Reagan as governor, and Robert H. Finch as lieutenant governor, will be in the best interests of California."

The long editorial made the following points:

Reagan has "steadfastly ignored attacks upon his personal integrity and personal motives," comporting "himself with dignity and courage in the face of brutal name-calling and guilt-by-association tactics."

Reagan has announced he will "draft the best brains in California" to assist him in drawing up programs in finance, law enforcement, agriculture, welfare and other complex areas.

Reagan has pledged himself to bring about "a more constructive relationship between government and business."

He has asserted he will replace welfare spending with "welfare investments" to rescue "discouraged men from the economic junkheap."

He approves the legitimate use of "Negro political and economic power," but not repressive "black power," to win deserved benefits.

He will solicit the best financial advice to devise a tax revision program.

It was a thoughtful editorial, one which the editors of the *Times*, an increasingly liberal although traditionally Republican paper, had obviously considered very carefully. They knew that what the *Times* said carried great weight. And so it did.*

In the last two weeks, both sides unleashed a television blitz, accounting for much of their $3 million election budgets. (This figure does not include the $3 million or so spent by labor on Brown.) The Brown forces scheduled 2,000 spot announcements on radio the next-to-last week and 2,500 spots the final week. On major TV stations there were 20 to 40 spots a week. The Reagan schedule included 400 TV spots up to one minute long during the next-to-last week, a five-minute program every night on each of the 13 key TV stations, and a one-hour "telethon" in San Francisco.

Labor tried desperately to counter-attack but even among blue-collar workers Ronald Reagan buttons could be found. One poll in mid-October showed that Reagan enjoyed 38% of the vote in the factories and mills populating the Los Angeles industrial complex. It must have been very frustrating, for as the labor editor of the Los Angeles *Herald Examiner* wrote: "In money and man-

---

* Other newspapers that endorsed Reagan included the Oakland *Tribune* (owned by former U.S. Senator William Knowland), San Jose *News* and San Diego *Union*.

power, unions have what must be a modern record invested in the fortunes of Pat Brown."

In one last desperate attempt to prove that there *was* a deliverable labor vote, Walter Reuther, president of the United Auto Workers and number two man in the AFL-CIO, came to town on October 28 to work some political magic. Reuther flourished all the old clichés: Reagan was "unreliable." "He sold out for 30 pieces of silver as the paid propagandist of General Electric." What happens on Nov. 8, the labor leader warned, will influence the bargaining posture of every union because "we do not operate in a vacuum."

Another visitor to California was to make far more difference: Stokely Carmichael, the leader of the Student Non-Violent Coordinating Committee, who spoke before 12,000 cheering students on the Berkeley campus of the University of California. If Reagan had a speechwriter and if this ghost had tried his very best, he could not have written a speech more calculated to help the GOP candidate.

On Oct. 29, nine short days before election day, Stokely declared that the only way to stop the war in Vietnam was for young Americans to say "to hell with the draft."

"And I am saying, 'To hell with the draft!'" he shouted. He added that the Vietnam war was "murder of women and kids" and that American Negro soldiers there are "nothing more than black mercenaries."

Significantly, Reagan had tried to prevent that which he must have suspected would be to his political benefit. He sent a telegram to Carmichael in New York asking him to cancel the trip and

"A PRAIRIE FIRE"

asked Brown to join him in the request. Caught in the middle again, Brown refused and lamely said he deplored Carmichael's appearance. Good old Pat Brown had done it again, or rather had *not* done anything again. Following his appearance, Brown condemned the SNCC leader's "to hell with the draft" speech and then added, incredibly enough: "Black power and the white backlash are now working strangely hand-in-glove to defeat me." Speaking on CBS-TV's *Face the Nation*, Reagan stated that he didn't think there was a white backlash in California "except in the mind of someone who wants to use it in a political sense." He added that if there was a backlash, it wasn't racial but only "a backlash against what seems to be a breakdown in law and order."

Still another visitor never arrived: President Lyndon Johnson, scheduled to spend two full days stumping California with the slumping Brown. However, after a two-week tour through Asia, a little summit meeting with our Asian allies in Manila, and a flying visit to the front in Vietnam, the President returned to the United States in very late October more tired than he cared to admit. It was announced, almost immediately, he was not going to campaign (it was even denied that he had ever planned to campaign although that was not true) but instead would be going into the hospital in a few days for minor surgery. Two weeks later he was operated on for removal of a noncancerous polyp from his throat and repair of an incisional hernia in his abdomen.

By now, Pat Brown wished that he too could go into the hospital, but he had the last few weary days of a frustrating campaign to endure.

The last Field Poll showed:
Reagan	46%
Brown	41%
Undecided	13%

The last State Poll reported:
Reagan	49%
Brown	43%
Undecided	8%

Brown said he found the figures "very encouraging." Reagan's managers, Bill Roberts and Phil Battaglia, tried to control their jubilation. It was obvious that, barring another San Francisco earthquake, their man was going to win by as much as 500,000 votes and maybe more.

On Monday, Nov. 7, the last day of the campaign, Brown flew from a breakfast rally in Los Angeles to a midday rally in San Francisco to a late afternoon event in San Jose. Reagan undertook a flying tour of six airport rallies from Sacramento to San Diego. The preceding Thursday he had been showered with confetti and cheered by thousands during a downtown parade in San Francisco—Pat Brown's home town. At every stop on that last day, the candidate cautioned the happy, sign-waving crowds against "over-confidence," asking them to turn out themselves as well as their friends and neighbors, in full force on the morrow.

They did.

Chapter Fifteen

LANDSLIDE II

The last polls showed Reagan five to six points ahead of Brown, with as many as 13% of the people undecided. The Reagan camp translated these figures into a very solid 500,000 plurality. Pat Brown stubbornly insisted that he would win by 300,000 votes—the memories of his 1,000,00 vote victory over William Knowland in 1958 and his 200,000 vote win over Richard Nixon in 1962 obviously etched in his mind. Brown's managers, clinging to outdated political clichés, expressed the hope that election day would bring "Democratic sunshine" and a large turnout which would help the governor because of the 3-2 registration edge Democrats enjoyed.

With the dawn of November 8, 1966, came cloudy, dripping skies over much of Southern California—which should have meant a lighter turnout and an advantage for the GOP. But, in fact, new voting records were set or threatened throughout the state with 79.19% of those Californians registered voting. By the old clichés, this should have meant a plus for the Democrats. But it was not to be in 1966 as Ronald Reagan and Company won every major state office but one, reduced the Democratic majorities in the Assembly and State Senate to prosciutto-thin margins and picked up three new Republican Congressmen.

The results of the gubernatorial contest:

| Ronald Reagan | 3,742,913 | 57% |
| Pat Brown | 2,749,174 | 42% |

It was a million vote victory, less 6,161. The Republican candidate carried 55 out of 58 counties, losing only Alameda (by less than 2,000), Plumas (by less than 100) and San Francisco, Pat Brown's home county (by about 50,000 votes). All three are in the North. Reagan piled up huge totals in Los Angeles County (over a 350,000 vote plurality), Orange County (a 180,000 vote plurality) and San Diego County (a 110,000 vote plurality). He received 60% of the Los Angeles vote and even 51% of the San Francisco Bay area vote, despite losing the city of San Francisco. Reagan garnered 57% of the votes of people with middle incomes—14% more than Nixon had in 1962. He received 65% of the non-Negro vote. As expected, Brown got an overwhelming 95% of the Negro vote but, according to pollster Don Muchmore, this was "not a significant change from 1962." Brown also got 76% of the Spanish-American vote, traditionally Democratic.

All observers agreed that Reagan's awesome margin was due to almost every one of the "undecideds" going for him rather than Brown. Clearly, Ronald Reagan had convinced them that he and his Creative Society would do more for California.

Other state-wide races:

For Lieutenant Governor:
Robert H. Finch (Rep.)   3,834,978
Glenn Anderson (Dem.)   2,578,887

Bob Finch, 41, campaign manager for Dick Nixon's presidential try in 1960, and campaign manager for George Murphy in his successful Senatorial drive in 1964, had been in trouble since the primary. Although popular with all shades of Republicans and many Democrats, Finch had not generated any appreciable enthusiasm. As the campaign entered its last month, some polls showed him 15% behind the lack-luster Anderson, who had handled so ineptly the Watts riot in 1965. But Reagan needed a *Republican* lieutenant governor whose duties in California go far beyond the usual ceremonial functions in most states. In the last three weeks, therefore, the campaign's emphasis was shifted to a Ronald Reagan—Bob Finch theme. Over $300,000 was spent on TV spots and billboards promoting the "team". Reagan and Finch campaigned together. When Reagan was not there, Senator Murphy was, calling on voters to back Finch. In addition, Finch had almost total newspaper support and it is generally agreed that editorial recommendations influence voters far more on lesser offices. A top campaign strategist told me flatly: "Finch would not have won without Reagan."*

---

* As can be seen, Finch received only 92,000 more votes than Reagan. His winning margin was much greater than Reagan's because his opponent, Anderson, pulled 171,000 less votes than Brown.

For Secretary of State:
Frank M. Jordan (Rep.)   3,481,016
Norbert S. Schlei (Dem.)   2,777,445

Jordan was an incumbent, having served as secretary of state for 24 years.

For Controller:
Houston L. Flournoy (Rep.) 3,186,455
Alan Cranston (Dem.)   3,125,070

Cranston, the man who had tried to present a JBS bouquet to Reagan, must have been particularly distressed to lose to Flournoy, a liberal professor-assemblyman.

For Treasurer:
Ivy Baker Priest (Rep.) *   3,203,367
Bert A. Betts (Dem.)   3,069,660

For Attorney General:
Thomas C. Lynch (Dem.)   3,375,334
Spencer Williams (Rep.)   2,901,840

Incumbent Lynch was the only Democrat to win a state-wide office. Pollster Muchmore attributed Williams' defeat to the fact that he trailed Lynch "by such a wide margin among those registered voters who characteristically vote." As they did for every other Republican, the bulk of the undecided's swung to Williams but they could not overcome Lynch's advantage among those who knew how they were going to vote. Williams was subsequently appointed Health and Welfare Administrator by Reagan.

In the state legislature, the Reagan landslide reduced the Democratic majority to two in the

---

* The attractive gray-haired Mrs. Priest was Treasurer of the United States under President Dwight D. Eisenhower.

Senate and four in the Assembly. Because of reapportionment, there were elections for all seats. The breakdown:

Before Nov. 8, 1966:
Senate   26 Democrats
               14 Republicans
Assembly   49 Democrats
               31 Republicans

After Nov. 8, 1966:
Senate   21 Democrats
               19 Republicans
Assembly   42 Democrats
               38 Republicans

In national offices, the Reagan sweep carried three new Republicans into Congress: Robert Mathias, former Olympic champion, Jerry Pettis, and Charles Wiggins. That they won because of Reagan can be seen in their winning percentages, which were 6%, 9% and 11%, respectively, behind the man at the top of the ticket. Reagan carried 31 out of 38 Congressional districts and received a greater percentage of the vote than the GOP candidate in 23 out of 38 districts. The new line-up was Democrats, 21 seats, Republicans, 17.

The governor-elect was elated, understandably, as were his campaign workers who jammed the Biltmore Bowl for a victory celebration. When Pat Brown conceded late Tuesday night, pandemonium ensued. As the band played, a surging crowd knocked over two policemen and a huge "Reagan for President" banner was unfurled.

The next day at a news conference, the governor-elect disavowed any Presidential ambitions but acknowledged that as the leader of a state with

40 electoral votes he would probably play a "significant" part in the 1968 national campaign. A few days later, when *U.S. News and World Report* asked if he would "object" if Republicans asked him to try for the Presidential nomination, Reagan replied:

"You dangle something there that is the supreme honor that can come to any citizen of the United States. Let me put it this way: I will do nothing to encourage such a thing. I will even discourage it, because I've been handed a great responsibility here as Governor of California, and I have nothing else in mind but getting at this job."

On election night, Reagan was asked about the meaning of his victory and replied: "It seems to be all over the country. The people seem to have shown that maybe we have moved too fast, and want to pause and reconsider the course we've been following."* Later for *U.S. News & World Report,* he became more specific:

"For me, the vote reflects the great concern of the people with the size and cost of government.

---

* President Johnson had predicted that there would be "minimal" Democratic losses in the House, if any losses at all, but in fact the 1966 elections were a nation-wide rejection of the Great Society. In the House, Republicans picked up a net gain of 47 seats. In the Senate, there was a net gain of three seats for the GOP. Republicans picked up a net of eight new governorships, bringing the count to 25 Republicans, 25 Democrats. But Republicans reigned in states with a total of 293 electoral votes—with 270 needed to elect a President. In the state legislatures, Republicans gained 677 seats, controlling both houses in 16 states, the Senate in 18 states and the lower house in another 22 states. Nationwide, Republicans received 54.1% of the popular vote, based on returns for Senate or Governor or for House seats where there were no statewide races. GOP analysts stated that one more election year like 1966—with its "minimal" losses for the Democrats—and LBJ would be back on the ranch, permanently.

"They were disturbed, too, by our runaway crime rate and the excessive cost of welfare. There was a belief that, as far as welfare is concerned, we were not curing the problem—weren't helping people to help themselves. We were just building up a whole segment of society that was coming along for a free ride.

"And, of course, the demonstrations and riots at the University of California at Berkeley had people deeply disturbed."

As a Republican governor with a Democratic legislature, he was asked, will you have trouble putting your program across? He replied:

"If you have a sound program that the legislators know will benefit the people, they will go along. We've got quite a record here in California of legislators crossing party lines for the good of the people."

Reagan sounded rather naive but within three days of his election, both Jesse Unruh, Speaker of the Assembly, and Attorney General Thomas Lynch, a Democrat, promised the Governor-elect their cooperation. Lynch specifically contradicted widely-circulated reports that he had hinted he might resign because of "white backlash" in the campaign. Lynch emphasized he had no such intention and that his only remark about backlash had been an offhand remark about not wanting to be associated with "white backlash" in *other* parts of the country.

As part of his running start to get at the job, Reagan appointed Phil Battaglia his executive secretary and A. C. Rubel chairman of a "Major Appointments Task Force," to screen prospective appointees to the more than 31 department directorships and 31 deputy directorships which constituted the bulk of the governor's patronage. Lyn Nofziger was made director of communications. Other staff appointments soon followed. A week later, after a very brief four-day vacation, Reagan spoke at an Associated Press Managing Editors convention in Coronado. There, the governor-elect asserted that he would consult with the people in his administration to bring about not centralized but grassroots government.

"The time has come," he said, stressing a by-now familiar theme, "to reimplement the original dream that resulted in the forming of this nation —the idea never fully tried in the world before— that you and I have the capacity for self-government—the dignity and the ability and God-given freedom to make our own decisions, plan our lives and control our destiny.

"People," he said, "would like a government that lectures less and listens more."

The job of his administration, he explained, "will be to provide the leadership and to restore to the people, through their city and county governments, the power and authority to solve those problems, or to share in their solution with the state government."

Could it be done? Did the people *want* it to be done after so many years of depending upon federal or state or local government to solve, if they could, all economic and social problems? Was Ronald Reagan the right man to undertake so monumental and revolutionary a task? Was *anybody* the right man?

One Reagan intimate suggested part of the answer when he said:

"This man will be the most unique political animal in history. Nobody has any strings on him."

It would take, assuredly, a man without strings, without obligations but with convictions and courage, to implement a Creative Society in a world seemingly ready to accept the proposition that that government is best which governs most.

PART THREE

THE GOVERNOR

Chapter Sixteen

"A CAUSE TO BELIEVE IN"

The tall, erect, sun-tanned man, immaculate in a dark blue suit and muted tie, waited for the waves of applause to subside. The sky was blue, the sun bright, the audience expectant. They had said he could not win the nomination. He had proved them wrong. They had said he could not win the general election. He had proved them wrong. Now they were saying that he could not govern. He intended to prove them wrong once again.

"To a number of us, this is a first and hence a solemn and momentous occasion, and yet, on the broad page of state and national history, what is taking place here is almost commonplace routine."

So Ronald Reagan, the 33rd governor of the state of California, began his inaugural address on the morning of January 5, 1967, on the West steps of the gold-domed State Capitol in Sacramento.

During his 27-minute speech, which was constantly interrupted by applause and several times by cheers, Governor Reagan outlined what he hoped he and the people would do together for their state. It was all based on the premise that "freedom is a fragile thing and is never more than one generation away from extinction. It is not ours by inheritance; it must be fought for and defended constantly by each generation."

The new governor asserted that "the path we will chart is not an easy one. It demands much of those chosen to govern, but also from those who did the choosing. And let there be no mistake about this: We have come to a crossroad—a time of decision—and the path we follow turns away from any idea that government and those who serve it are omnipotent.

"It is a path impossible to follow unless we have faith in the collective wisdom and genius of the people. Along this path government will lead but not rule, listen but not lecture. It is the path of a Creative Society."

He did not confine himself to rounded generalities but offered pointed proposals:

"We will propose legislation to give to local communities the right to pass and enforce ordinances which will enable the police to more adequately protect these communities.

"I pledge my support and fullest effort to a plan which will remove from politics, once and for all, the appointment of judges.*

"We can and must frame legislation . . . to protect (our young people) from the . . . harmful effects of exposure to smut and pornography.

"Lawlessness by the mob, as with the individual, will not be tolerated. We will act firmly and quickly to put down riot or insurrection wherever and whenever the situation requires.

"We seek reforms that will, wherever possible, change relief check to paycheck. . . . (But) only private industry in the last analysis can provide jobs with a future. Lieut. Gov. Robert Finch will

---

* Before he left his Sacramento office in late December, 1966, lame-duck Governor Brown filled 80 vacancies on the California judicial bench.

be liaison between government and the private sector in an all-out program of job training and education leading to real employment.

"On the subject of education . . . hundreds of thousands of young men and women will receive an education in our state colleges and universities.

"We are proud of our ability to provide this opportunity for our youth and we believe it is no denial of academic freedom to provide this education within a framework of reasonable rules and regulations. Nor is it a violation of individual rights to require obedience to these rules and regulations or to insist that those unwilling to abide by them should get their education elsewhere."

The audience of nearly 20,000 erupted into loud applause and cheers. Berkeley was 90 miles away.

"It seems to me that government must accept a responsibility for safe-guarding each union member's democratic rights within his union. For that reason we will submit legislative proposals to guarantee each union member a secret ballot in his union on policy matters and the use of union dues."

At last he came to the most tangled problem of all—the cost of government—and he told the thousands before him and the millions watching him on television and listening to him on radio the uncompromising truth: the state of California was in serious financial trouble. The budget for the year ending July, 1967, was $4.6 billion and despite a bookkeeping gimmick of using 15 months revenue there would still be a deficit of $63 million. The budget for 1967-68 would be several hundred million dollars more and with "projected increases plus funding for property tax relief which I believe is absolutely essential . . . our deficit in the coming year would reach three-quarters of a billion dollars. . . ."

Reagan gave it to them cold-turkey: "We are going to squeeze and cut and trim until we reduce the cost of government. It won't be easy, nor will it be pleasant, and it will involve every department of government, starting with the governor's office."

Nor did he rule out the possibility of taxes, saying that he would turn to "additional sources of revenue . . . if it becomes clear that economies alone cannot balance the budget."

He exhorted the people to join with him, explaining, "This is not just a problem for the administration; it is a problem for all of us to solve together. I know that you can face any prospect and do anything that has to be done as long as you know the truth of what you are up against. . . ."

The new governor paused and looked behind and above him.

"If, in glancing aloft, some of you were puzzled by the small size of our state flag . . . there is an explanation. That flag was carried into battle in Vietnam by young men of California. Many will not be coming home. One did—Sergeant Robert Howell, grievously wounded. He brought that flag back. I thought we would be proud to have it fly over the Capitol today. It might even serve to put our problems in better perspective. It might remind us of the need to give our sons and daughters a cause to believe in and banners to follow."

A veteran legislator seated on the broad platform whispered to a friend: "By God, he's going

"A CAUSE TO BELIEVE IN"

to do *exactly* what he said he was during the campaign!"

But first there was a four-day "fiesta," which included the dramatic oath-taking ceremony shortly after midnight, January 2, in the rotunda of the Capitol; a San Francisco Symphony concert; a prayer breakfast; a civic luncheon given by the Sacramento Chamber of Commerce, and a grand ball at the State Fairgrounds, which attracted more than 5,000 people. Explained Richard (Sandy) Quinn, who coordinated the many activities, "Governor Reagan wanted an inauguration that would *establish* some traditions for the first state in the nation." The New York *Times* summed up: "Never before, observers of the political scene said today, has a Governor been inaugurated so thoroughly and with such pageantry." The governor clearly liked Quinn's coordination for he appointed the 31-year-old former press secretary to Senator George Murphy his appointments secretary. Quinn later became Phil Battaglia's assistant.

At the ball, comedian Danny Thomas introduced the governor by saying: "The people of California have given you a four-year contract. And if it pleases God, it will be renewed and I hope the residuals are wonderful."

By then, Reagan had begun to grapple with the residuals of the Brown Administration, which were *far* from wonderful.

The budget estimates given the new administration by the old administration called for expenditures of $4.8 billion, *excluding any new programs*, for the fiscal year starting July 1, 1967. Revenues were divided in this manner: $3.2 billion from the general fund, which finances most of the state's operating activities; $1.1 billion from "special funds," intended for such things as highway construction and wild-life conservation; and $519 million from funds raised through bond issues to finance California's water project, construction at the University of California and similar projects.

There was an estimated gap of $500 million between revenues and expenditures in the general fund. Cash in the special and bond funds could *not* legally be used to fill the general fund gap. The new administration had to act, and fast, because it was required by state law to submit its budget to the state legislature by no later than January 31—less than four weeks away. Although the new director of finance, Gordon Smith (a former vice president with the well-known management firm, Booz, Allen and Hamilton), had been analyzing the budget since early December, he and his team were unfamiliar with many of the intricacies of the state budget. More time was what they needed and did not have.

At first glance, it might seem no arduous task to trim drastically a $3.2 billion general fund budget. But almost two-thirds of this sum was payments made to counties and communities for such activities as public education and welfare. Most of these subsidies, as *Fortune* magazine pointed out, "were required either by provisions in the state constitution or by statute, and could not be reduced without repealing existing laws."

Any trimming in this area was also blocked by the firm promise Reagan made during the campaign that he would provide *more* state assistance to local governments so that they could reduce property taxes—the major source of their income.

"A CAUSE TO BELIEVE IN"

The state's 3,700,000 homeowners had huzzahed Reagan for his commitment to reduce the nation's highest property taxes. He could not now ignore that commitment, which he would do if he attempted to reduce state subsidies.

What was left, then, on which the budget cutter could practice his skill? About $1.15 billion in the state government's operating expenses. The two largest items were $464 million for higher education (chiefly at the University of California and state colleges) and $193 million for care of the mentally ill. They were sacred cows invariably revered by all, but Reagan and his advisers were determined to practice austerity, no matter what happened. And almost everything did.

The University of California had requested a record $278 million for 1967-68. Gordon Smith and his budget team recommended that this be cut by $82 million—more than 25% of the total. A good part of the difference, Reagan suggested, about $20 million, should be made up by charging annual tuition for Californians (out of state students already paid tuition of close to $1000 annually). The governor's proposed tuition was $250 to $280 for the University of California and $150 to $160 for the state colleges.* In addition, he asked the U.C. board of regents to use the $20 million contingency fund to pay some of the university's bills.

If Ronald Reagan had dropped an H-bomb on Berkeley he could not have enraged the academic

* At his first news conference as governor on January 10, Reagan said: "There is no such thing as *free* education. The question is who pays? I think there is nothing wrong with young people being responsible for a part of the cost." He suggested that some "who come to agitate, not to study," might have second thoughts about demonstrations if they invested their money in tuition.

community more. U.C. President Clark Kerr flew back immediately from a trip in the Far East to declare that any such cut would force the university to turn away 22,400 qualified students from its nine campuses in September.* Franklin Murphy, chancellor of the University of California at Los Angeles (UCLA), normally thought of as friendly to the new administration, said: "I must state plainly that I do not intend to preside at the liquidation or substantial erosion of the quality which fifty years of effort have created at UCLA." The governor was hanged in effigy at Fresno State College, his home in Pacific Palisades was picketed, and protest rallies were held, among other locales, at Long Beach State College, Valley State College and San Jose State College.

On January 20, the U.C. Board of Regents met for the first time under the Reagan administration. They deferred action on tuition and displayed little interest in reducing the budget request. But they *did* fire Clark Kerr as president of the University of California by a vote of 14 to 8. Another H-Bomb had been dropped with Ronald Reagan widely assumed to be the bombardier who pressed the release button.

While it is true that Reagan was sharply critical of Kerr during the gubernatorial race, it is *not* true

---

* Less than two years earlier, the California Coordinating Council for Higher Education (*including Clark Kerr among its members*) concluded that the policy of free tuition at all state institutions ought to be changed. A major reason for the finding was that 20% of the students at the University of California come from households with an annual income between $14,000 and $20,000. Another 18% come from families whose income exceeds $20,000 annually. It was clearly unreasonable to ask the California taxpayer to help subsidize the education of those who could pay their own way.

"A CAUSE TO BELIEVE IN"

that he led a Board of Regents vendetta against the U.C. president. In the first place, the Board of Regents had almost fired Kerr two years before because of his indecisive handling of Mario Savio and the Free Speech Movement at Berkeley. Only Governor Brown's personal intervention at that time had saved Kerr.

Secondly, the board was made up of 24 prominent Californians—16 of whom had been appointed by Governor Brown and Goodwin Knight (this group voted 9 to 5 for dismissal). The other eight were members of the board because of their public office. They were: Governor Reagan, Lt. Gov. Robert Finch, Assembly Speaker Jesse Unruh, State School Superintendent Max Rafferty, State Agriculture Board President Allan Grant, Theodore R. Meyer, president of the San Francisco Mechanics Institute, and chairman of the Board of Regents, Harry R. Haldeman, president of the University's alumni association, and Clark Kerr.

Two members were absent and did not vote: Max Rafferty and Clark Kerr.

Late Friday night, January 20, following the firing of Clark Kerr, Reagan stated that "the matter of a vote of confidence was brought up by Dr. Kerr, not the board. His request came as a complete surprise to all of us."

The following day, Kerr retorted: "The governor's statement is completely false. I never have asked for a vote of confidence and I didn't yesterday."

Somebody was lying—or standing on their semantic rights.

Board chairman Meyer set the record quite straight on January 23, although his statement has not received the attention it should from academicians more eager to cry "McCarthyism!" than to find the truth. Here is what Mr. Meyer said, as reported in the New York *Times:*

"Dr. Kerr's status has been the subject of discussion and speculation for several years. His relations with the Regents were adversely affected by his handling of the Berkeley campus disorders in the fall of 1964. They deteriorated further as a result of his action the following spring in announcing his intended resignation to the press without consulation with or notice to any of the Regents. Some subsequent events did not improve the relationship. The resulting uncertainty and controversy have been harmful to the university in many ways."

Before the January 20 meeting, Meyer said, he and Mrs. Dorothy Chandler, the board's vice chairman, met with Dr. Kerr *at the president's request* (emphasis added).

"He told us," said Meyer, "that he could not carry on effectively under existing conditions, and that if the question of his continuance in office was likely to come up at any board meeting in the near future, he thought the Regents should face up to it and *decide it now one way or the other* (emphasis added)."

Meyer said that he and Mrs. Chandler asked Dr. Kerr whether he would be willing to resign, and the reply was no. Following the 14-8 vote "to terminate Dr. Kerr's services as President," Meyer and Mrs. Chandler again visited Dr. Kerr. They told him of the vote and of the Regents' "hope that before it was made public he would reconsider his refusal to resign.

"He said that he would not do so and that the board must take the responsibility. Under these circumstances, the question whether Dr. Kerr requested a 'vote of confidence' or a 'clarification of his status' appears to be *more a question of semantics than one of substance* (emphasis added)."

In addition, Mrs. Randolph Hearst, another regent and wife of the newspaper publisher, said, "Kerr delivered an ultimatum to the Regents to the effect that they must either give him a vote of confidence or release him from the office of president. . . . This action was initiated in no way by the Regents."

Dr. Kerr did not call Meyer or Mrs. Chandler or Mrs. Hearst liars nor challenge their public statements, although he did continue to insist that he was a victim of "politics."

Indeed, he was—his own.*

In the meantime, Reagan and his team pressed on with their austerity program. The governor called on all state agencies to begin implementing a 10% reduction in their operating budgets and he imposed a freeze on all state hiring to halt replacements or additions to California's 165,000 civil service employees.

"No department can expect to have a free ride," he declared. "We are running tens of millions of dollars behind the budget that was approved for the present fiscal year ending June 30. . . . We are in the way a family sometimes gets—outgo is

---

* It was later reported that *before* his removal as president, Clark Kerr had accepted the part-time chairmanship of the Carnegie Study of the Future of Higher Education, a project expected to take three or four years to complete. In this context, Kerr could force a vote of "confidence" or "status," knowing that he had a first-rate job waiting for him. An anticlimactic note: on April 10, it was announced that Kerr would take a part-time teaching and research post at Berkeley in the fall of 1967.

far in excess of income. We just kid ourselves if we go on with a kind of fiscal sleight of hand."

On January 31, Governor Reagan submitted to the legislature a 1967-68 budget of $4.615 billion—down about $250,000,000, or 5%, from what he estimated the state would have spent by the end of the current fiscal year, ending June 30, 1967. Despite the cutbacks, he said that California would still face a deficit of $240 to $250 million. He added he would submit tax increase proposals shortly.

The night before, in a televised "Report to the People," Reagan declared that under Pat Brown the state "had been looted and drained of its financial resources in a manner unique in our history. Not since the bleak days of the Depression," he charged, "when California was forced to such desperate measures our credit was affected for decades—have we faced such a dark picture." He reported that "California, for the last year, has been spending $1 million a day more than it has been taking in."

Reagan added that new or increased taxes in the amount of $240 million would be needed "just to balance the budget . . . if all the economies we've proposed are put into effect."

Democrats in Sacramento were shocked—by the governor's use of the shibboleth, "looted," and his talk about a tax increase. Assembly Leader Jesse Unruh, who had derided Brown in private and in public for years, allowed as how he was "very distressed" about the governor's language. "The governor," he said piously, "certainly couldn't have meant the dictionary application of the word, 'looting.' That implies criminality. I certainly *hope* that isn't what he meant."

"A CAUSE TO BELIEVE IN"

At his weekly news conference, Reagan expressed regret at having used the word "looted," describing himself as "addicted" to using the simplest words instead of terms such as "profligate" in his public speeches. He admitted that it was a "bad choice of words . . . and I'm sorry; I do not mean to imply any criminality."

But he insisted on making his point: The state was "going in the hole" financially, money had been spent and the fact "that the money was nonexistent was concealed from the people."

The determined Reagan administration continued to apply the brakes of the toboggan, effecting savings in large and small ways and, even more important, doing their utmost to convince the state employees that they meant it.

In the first six months, for example, the new administration:

(1) Sold the *Grizzly II*, the state Convair used by Brown, for $217,000, and ordered state officials to travel by commercial plane.

(2) Reduced out-of-state travel by state officials and employees by 74%.

(3) Froze purchase of new automobiles and equipment by department heads and consolidated motor-pool operations for a 15% saving in gasoline buying.

(4) Banned fancy-colored brochures and reports by departments and ordered them to use mimeograph machines. (Savings: $550,000 annually.)

(5) Scheduled the closing of eight of the state's 41 conservation camps, centers for fighting fire and erosion.

(6) Reduced the state civil service by 2,550 full-time employees (out of a total of 165,000).

(7) Canceled a proposed 10-story office building (cost: $4 million) as "unnecessary."

(8) Eliminated $750,000 from the budget for a new governor's mansion. A private group is raising the funds to build an official governor's mansion in accord with the principles of the Creative Society. The Governor and Mrs. Reagan moved out of the old mansion on March 1, 1967, for a simple reason: it was a fire trap.

(9) Initiated a review of telephone use which is expected to save $2 million annually.

Many state agencies reported sizeable cuts in their annual budgets. The office of Consumer Counsel reduced its budget by 77%. Other offices were not so successful. The state supreme court could only cut its budget $5000, $129,000 less than the economy goal assigned it. State colleges cut their budget $4 million, $33 million less than what the administration had hoped to effect.

One major obstacle in the way of the Creative Society was the attitude of the state's bureaucracy, typified in this comment by an old Sacramento hand to a *Fortune* reporter: "We have been through this kind of thing before, though never quite so deep a cut. What you do is make temporary cuts in your operating expenses, while keeping your crews and your equipment intact. That way you can hold down costs for a single year, while making no real reduction in your program."

What the old hands didn't realize was that Ronald Reagan was serious about Operation Austerity—it was not a publicity gimmick, nor was his suggestion that state employees volunteer to work without extra compensation on Lincoln's and Washington's Birthdays, thus saving the state about $7 million. However, the proposal went

"A CAUSE TO BELIEVE IN"

over like a wooden (George Washington) nickel. Union leaders protested. The Democratic-controlled legislature took a long-weekend holiday, including Lincoln's Birthday, although Assembly Speaker Jesse Unruh and Senate President Pro Tem Hugh Burns, both Democrats, agreed at their weekly news conference that there was nothing wrong with inviting state employees to work on holidays. Said Burns: "I could think of many requests that would be much worse than working one day on a holiday. For instance, a cut in pay . . ." Only a tiny percentage of the 165,000 state employees showed up on the two holidays, but Governor Reagan had made his point with the public, most of whom *did* work on Lincoln's and Washington's Birthdays.

In late March, the governor submitted a revised budget for 1967-68 of $5.06 billion—$434 million more than he had asked for in January. Of this $440 million increase, $170 million represented the first installment on his promise to expand state aid to local districts, providing relief to payers of property taxes. Another $75 million resulted from the unexpected rise in Medi-Cal costs (Medi-Cal is the state's program which provides medical care for indigents under 65 in collaboration with the federal Medicare law). Total expenditures came to $184 million more than the actual spending under Pat Brown's last budget—"the smallest increase," as Minority Leader Robert Monagan put it, "in any year since I have been in office." It represented an 8% increase over the 1966-67 budget which had been 16% higher than the preceding year's.

To acquire the needed extra revenue and balance the budget, Governor Reagan called for a tax increase of $946 million. He tapped just about everyone, proposing raises in personal income taxes, the sales tax, excise tax on cigarets and liquor as well as raises in the tax on corporate net profits and on banks. Reagan, the alleged captive of Big Business, "could not have gone any heavier on bank and corporate income taxes," conceded former Finance Director Hale Champion, a liberal Democrat.

Reagan also added $38 million to the appropriation for higher education—with some $20 million going to the University of California. That meant a total of $216.5 million for U.C.—a figure which was raised to $230.1 million in the final budget version. The Regents added another $20 million from the contingency fund.

In his original message of January 31, Reagan had proposed 10% cuts in operating expenses for almost all state agencies. His March message restored about $55 million of that money but left a reduction in operating expenses of $127 million— "the largest economy accomplished in the history of California state government," Reagan maintained. It was over 8 per cent, not a bad performance by an administration which was told it couldn't be done.*

In mid-March, Operation Austerity collided with the last remaining program in which substantial savings could be made: the Department of Mental Hygiene. Reagan announced that nearly 3,000

---

* In August, Reagan used his shears once again by trimming $200 million from Medi-Cal for 1967-68, explaining that the program had run up a deficit of $130 million during its first 16 months. The governor emphasized that no basic health and life-saving services were eliminated, and that the program would still pay out $600 million to about 1.5 million needy Californians.

positions in the mental hospitals and elsewhere in the department would be eliminated and that eight mental health clinics would be closed. Annual savings to the state: $20 million.

The outcry was almost louder and longer than that raised about the firing of Clark Kerr in January. There were references to "the Snake Pit" and "the Middle Ages." But the governor's staff had discovered that the patient population in the state's mental hospitals had declined 40% in the last four years and there had been *no* comparable reduction in hospital personnel. Critics replied that the 40% reduction in patient population had not resulted in a like reduction in work load. Under the proposed new standards, they argued, staffing would be only 67% adequate for the mentally ill and 63% for the mentally retarded. The sum of $100,000 was sought to pay for anti-Reagan TV commercials and newspaper ads. Newspapers sympathetic to Reagan began wavering. The Los Angeles *Times,* however, backed the governor describing his economy move "as a step in the right direction—and one that makes abundant good sense." But a poll showed that 58% of the public opposed the governor's economy stand on mental health, while only 23% favored it.

As a result, the closing of five clinics was put off for one year. The Department of Mental Hygiene, the governor announced, had full authority to halt all cuts "if at any time it appears that patient care will suffer."

The mental health issue might have damaged Reagan and his drive for economy badly if it had not been for a 15 minute "Report to the People" carried over 22 TV stations in California. His explanation of why he had reduced the staff of the

Department of Mental Hygiene neutralized much of the antagonism. Although it did not swing a majority over to his side, his report convinced the people once again that Ronald Reagan was doing *his* best to represent *their* best interests.

On June 30, Deadline Day, Governor Reagan signed a budget for 1967-68 of $5.07 billion—the largest state budget in U.S. history. At the very last moment, he trimmed $43.5 million from such departments as the University of California, state colleges and mental hygiene. Although there had been protests and sarcastic remarks about the "economies" of the Creative Society, the Senate approved the budget by 31-8, the Assembly by 64-15. The wide margins reflected the increasingly persuasive voice of the new governor.

A month later, Reagan signed a $900-plus million tax bill which was the largest state tax increase in U.S. history. The money was needed to balance the budget, pay off a $194 million debt left over from the previous administration and finance a reduction in property taxes for elderly homeowners—a modest $25 million start on his promise to provide relief for all owners.

Unruh and other Democratic leaders had earlier suggested that income taxes be deducted directly from paychecks but Reagan successfully opposed this move toward withholding. He insisted that taxpayers should be kept "painfully" aware of the cost of government by paying their income tax once a year.

In signing the tax bill, the governor emphasized that "the people of California are still paying too much for government, but I'm optimistic that in the next year we can reduce the cost of government."

"A CAUSE TO BELIEVE IN"

Throughout his first year in Sacramento, Reagan did not flinch, regardless of the issue.

For four years, Pat Brown postponed executions in the hope that capital punishment would be abolished by the state legislature. No action was taken and when Ronald Reagan took office there were 60 convicts waiting to be led into the gas chamber. Amid midnight vigils and passionate speeches, the new governor declined to stay the execution of Aaron Mitchell, who died on April 12. Reagan explained that the death penalty is a deterrent to capital crimes and that until the courts acted he would be obliged to obey the law. Soon thereafter the courts stayed the sentences of the next two men scheduled for execution.

As liberal columnist Roscoe Drummond wrote: "This is another example showing that, however much one may disagree with him, Reagan thinks for himself and is capable of standing by his own decisions whatever the political pressures."

Equally controversial was the bill liberalizing the state's abortion laws. Emphasizing that the bill was "by no means perfect," Reagan reluctantly signed it on June 16. The statute legalizes abortions when the child's birth would endanger the physical or mental health of the mother, in cases of statutory rape involving a girl under 15 years of age, and when pregnancy resulted from forcible rape or incest. The statute replaced one that permitted abortions only to save the mother's life. The bill passed the Assembly by 48-30 and the Senate by 21-17 after considerable pressure had been brought to bear against its passage by the Catholic Church and other organizations.

Clark Kerr, taxes, the budget, mental hospitals, capital punishment, abortion laws, *Grizzly II*—

all these dramatic issues were the visible tip of the iceberg. Beneath the waterline, invisible and generally unknown to the public, was the far greater part of the Creative Society. Much of it revolved around nearly 200 businessmen, on loan for six months from their companies and corporations, who were probing every aspect of state government, seeking to improve the efficiency and economy of operations. These men, all executives with salaries up to $100,000 a year, were donating their time. They were living in cramped hotel rooms in Sacramento and other cities throughout the state. One group was studying California's tax structure. Another was checking buying and housekeeping practices at state institutions. Another was inquiring into state relief rolls and alleged "welfare frauds."

Their examinations and recommendations would determine in great measure the success or failure of Ronald Reagan's belief that "government *can* be run by the people and run with common sense answers to the problems of government and run with common sense business practices."

Was such government possible in the modern America of the 1960's? Equally important, did the people *want* such government?

Chapter Seventeen

OF, BY AND FOR THE PEOPLE

Ronald Reagan needed the following to implement his revolutionary concept (revolutionary, that is, for California after eight years of Pat Brown) of *better*, not more government: (a) a knowledgeable, hard-working personal staff; (b) top flight executives, not political appointees, as heads of the various state agencies; (c) the cooperation or at least the non-hostility of the state legislature; and (d) the understanding and backing of the people of California. Throw in the Aegean Stables and you have enough work for a Hercules. Although he has made mistakes, Reagan has done a remarkable job for anyone, amateur or professional politician, in putting together the above elements.

First, his own personal staff. The same two men who were his closest advisers during the campaign remain his most trusted aides today: Phil Battaglia and Lyn Nofziger. The governor calls Battaglia "my strong right arm." He has to be, for the 32-year-old executive secretary starts work in the governor's suite of offices at 8 a.m. and often winds up at midnight, having attended working luncheons and dinners along the way. Visitors and phones occupy most of his day until 5:30 p.m., when on Monday, Wednesday, and Friday, an "inner cabinet" meeting is held. In attendance (besides the governor) are Communications Director Nofziger, William P. Clark, Jr., cabinet secretary, and the four executive directors: Spencer Williams, Health and Welfare; Norman Livermore, State Resources; Gordon Luce, Transportation; and Earl Coke, Agriculture. Battaglia is the youngest of a young cabinet which averages 46.5 years.

From 7:30 to 9 p.m. or so, the executive secretary often confers with the governor at the temporary mansion, located in a Sacramento suburb. If not, he may dine with staff members like Sandy Quinn, his assistant, at restaurants near the Capitol —holding dinner-conferences which rarely end before midnight.

Battaglia is a lawyer who first entered politics in 1962 when he campaigned for Sen. Thomas Kuchel and Richard Nixon. He became active in the Los Angeles Chamber of Commerce, and was elected president in 1965.

Says Battaglia of his boss, whom he first met in late 1965, "My admiration for him grows every day." Asked about the criticisms aimed at the Reagan administration, the husky, balding politico replies: "As a student of politics, I've learned that the only one who keeps everybody happy doesn't get the job done." *

Lyn Nofziger was one of the best-liked and most

* In late August, Battaglia announced that he was returning to the private practice of law but would be "happy to help" Governor Reagan "in any way he saw fit to ask me." The governor responded that Battaglia's "brilliance and his leadership are responsible for much of what this administration has been able to accomplish.

"However, I have known from the beginning that his service would be limited and that he would have to return to his profession. I wish him Godspeed."

quoted political reporters in Washington, D.C., where he worked for the Copley newspapers of California and Illinois. As communications director for Governor Reagan, Nofziger remains a shirt-sleeves, cigar-smoking, wise-cracking guy but with one significant difference of course—he is now giving rather than getting news. As he admits, "the problem is sometimes there is a conflict of interest between what the press wants and what I think they should have." Nofziger has two aides: Paul Beck, a former reporter for the Los Angeles *Times*, who holds the title of press secretary, and Nancy Clark Reynolds, a very attractive specialist in radio and television who worked for a San Francisco TV station. Another hard-working aide is omni-competent Judith Kernoff, the assistant press secretary. In addition to coordinating the communications of the Reagan administration, Nofziger is constantly in conference with the governor—at breakfasts, lunches, dinners and in between. He and Battaglia have the only two keys to Reagan's private office in the corner of the Capitol. If Battaglia is the governor's strong right arm then Nofziger is his equally strong left arm—although the former newspaperman is more conservative than the lawyer.

Still another key aide is 35-year-old Bill Clark, cabinet secretary and coordinator of the thrice weekly "inner cabinet" meeting. Its procedures reflect his logical, precise mind and personality. Clark, Battaglia and the four executive directors prepare one page memorandums on the issues to be covered. They are divided into four parts: issue, facts, discussion (pro and con), and recommendation. They must be one page, no more and no less. At first, Clark has acknowledged, there were frequent objections that complicated topics could not be condensed to one page.

"But it has been found that almost any issue can be reduced to a single page," he says. "At times if the governor wants to go into the thing in more depth, he will request more detailed reports. He's a late-night reader."

Generally, eight to twelve issues are taken up in each 30-minute period with Reagan making a decision then and there. Clark lauds the governor's "incisive" manner. "He has the ability," the cabinet secretary asserts, "to digest material quickly and to ask vital questions. More often than not, he puts what has become his trademark around here— 'OK, RR'—on the bottom of the memos. I take the originals and they are filed in our minutes book."

To those who criticize the system, Clark replies simply: "Everyone wants to see the Governor, but the only way he can operate efficiently is to ration his time. Otherwise, chaos would exist."

The executive directors who meet with the governor are:

- Spencer Williams, 44, administrator of health and welfare, and the only Republican who failed to win his statewide office (attorney general) the previous fall. Departments under his wing include Public Health, Mental Hygiene, Rehabilitation, Social Welfare, Corrections, Employment, Industrial Relations, Veterans Affairs, and the California Youth Authority.

- Norman Livermore, Jr., 55, a lumber company executive, administrator of state resources. Departments under him include Water Resources, Fish and Game, Parks and Recreation, Harbors and Watercraft, Conservation, Bay Area Transportation Study Commission, Housing and the State Office of Planning.

- Gordon C. Luce, 41, former San Diego savings and loan official, administrator of transportation and business. His departments include General Services, Alcoholic Beverage Control, Banking, Corporations, Real Estate, Savings and Loan, Insurance, Professional Standards, the Public Utilities Commission and the State Personnel Board and Retirement System.

Says the always articulate Luce about the Creative Society: "The longer this administration is here the more cost-cutting will be possible without impairing essential services.

"The business approach to government has been tried in other states, but we just happen to be the biggest. . . . It's something the country is watching. What we are accomplishing is something other states can accomplish too."

- Earl Coke, 66, who reorganized the U.S. Department of Agriculture in the 1950's, administrator of agriculture. Although not originally included, Coke was elevated to the inner cabinet in recognition of the fact that farming is the state's leading industry.

Brown had eight agency chiefs overseeing the state's 23 departments. Reagan has reduced their number to four at the suggestion, among others, of Richard Krabach, Ohio's finance director, who told the new administration how Ohio had cut 5000 jobs and lowered state costs 9% after GOP Governor James A. Rhodes took office.

Luce, Williams, Livermore, and Coke are business executives who earned far more in the world of business than they are presently making in state government. Reagan's finance director, Gordon Smith, commanded a salary of more than $100,000 a year. His state salary is $30,000—a sizeable pay cut. These men reflect the determination of the Reagan administration to put $100,000-a-year men into $25,000-a-year jobs—not to fill top state posts with people who would like a 100% salary increase at the state's expense. Such officials also reflect Reagan's ability to persuade outstanding men and women to make sizeable personal sacrifices toward the goal of a better California.

Perhaps the most important of them all is H. C. (Chad) McClellan, a Los Angeles businessman, who resigned as president of his paint company to become head of a non-profit organization called the Management Council for Merit Employment Training and Research.

What he has done is truly remarkable. McClellan persuaded more than 2,600 companies in the Los Angeles area to cooperate in a job-training and job-finding program for residents of Watts, the same Watts which erupted into such terrible violence in 1965. At that time, statistics showed about 25,000 unemployed people in Watts. Immediately following the riots, McClellan, a former president of the Los Angeles Chamber of Commerce, swung into action and within 18 months, 17,500 unemployed had private enterprise jobs. Here was the Creative Society in action.

One of Governor Reagan's first acts was to ask Chad McClellan to extend his operations throughout California. At no cost to the state (the program is funded by individuals and foundations) McClellan now has "skill centers" which provide short-time training for factory employees in Los

Angeles and is setting up similar centers in San Diego, the San Francisco Bay area and Fresno. Chad McClellan is a most unusual man, as revealed in this story about a meeting between the Los Angeles businessman and a hundred young Negroes from Watts, which Reagan likes to tell:

"McClellan appeared personally before that group of young men. Everyone had a jail record—young men who admitted they had led in the riots but had turned around and organized themselves actually to curb disorder in the future. And this was a group of fellows who, if you sent them to Vietnam, you would not have to send weapons. McClellan challenged them to take jobs. Of the 100 of them, 82 accepted the challenge.

"And today they are working in private enterprise jobs with records of no tardiness, no absenteeism. Some of them even are moving up with promotions."

As columnist Victor Riesel put it: "The governor sees the business community—and not the federal government—as the salvation of the Negro community—from Watts to Harlem."

The man directly responsible for this key program in the Creative Society is Lt. Gov. Robert Finch. Although critics of Reagan persist in saying otherwise, Finch is one of the most important men in the Reagan administration. The most obvious proof is Finch's liaison between the governor and Chad McClellan.

In addition, the two men have lunch together every week—usually on Wednesday—to discuss programs and strategy. Finch also meets at least once a week with the governor's top aides—Battaglia and Nofziger. Admittedly less conservative than

Reagan, Bob Finch serves a highly important function as middle-man between the governor and various groups on critical issues.

Finch and Richard Cornuelle, author of *Reclaiming the American Dream* and the concept of Independent Action,* attended the same California college. Because of the philosophical similarities between the Creative Society and Independent Action, Finch set up a meeting in August, 1966 between the governor and his old college friend so that they could exchange ideas and theories. The two men keep in contact.

As lieutenant governor, Finch spends at least one day a week in his Los Angeles office, makes from 20 to 30 speeches a month, serves on the University of California Board of Regents, the Board of Trustees of the State College System, is a member of the State Lands Commission and chairman of the International Commission of the Californias.

A San Francisco reporter summed it up laconically: "The job isn't confined to waiting for a gubernatorial vacancy or a chance to break a tie vote in the Senate."

Reagan is making effective and continuing use

---

* Independent Action is based on the activities of what Cornuelle calls the Independent Sector, composed of thousands of private institutions like foundations, churches, civic organizations, clubs and unions plus the individual efforts of 200 million Americans. The Independent Sector was the driving force behind much of America's social progress for 150 years. Private organizations dug canals, built schools, started seminaries, erected hospitals, helped the poor, cared for the sick and the elderly, supported missionaries, printed books, made movies —in short, solved public problems of an endless variety without looking for assistance to the state capitol, let alone Washington, D. C.

of his lieutenant governor who is almost as good a bet as he was to be governor some day.

As might be expected, not everybody agreed that Reagan appointees were remarkable—or suited for government.

One outgoing Brown official commented: "The new men are either stuffy business types who think nobody in the state knows anything, or eager beaver Chamber of Commerce types just itching to learn everything they can."

"The governor has surrounded himself with a bunch of nice young men," said a Democratic senator, "none with a day's worth of practical experience in politics."

Members of the state legislature were particularly critical of Reagan's closest advisers in the early months. "Whiz kids!" snorted one Republican Assemblyman.

As one political editor wrote: "Legislators are extremely sensitive about their role in government and insist—rightly so—that the legislative branch is fully equal to the executive branch."

This understandably proud attitude of the legislature was reinforced by the passage of Proposition 1A in November, 1966. Included in its provisions were a salary raise to $16,000, a tax-free expense account of $175 a week while the legislature was in session and no limit on the length of the session. For the first time in its history, California was to have a full-time legislature with members who were legislators, not party hacks or representatives of special interests. As the San Francisco *Chronicle* commented: "It is a busy and lively body with an unusually high proportion of talented men and women."

There was another reason why, in the first few months, the Reagan administration suffered from poor liaison with the legislature: an unprecedented flood of work. For example, under the Brown administration an average of 600 to 800 letters a day were received in the governor's office. The daily average in March, 1967, was *6,000* letters. Furthermore, the inner secretariat had been cut back in January from Brown's 90 people—with 15 more borrowed from various departments—to 75. Since then more secretaries have been added to handle the work flow. Liaison is running smoothly. In early May, a top Republican legislator admitted: "The whole operation is improving now."

The improvement was no accident. As he always has, Ronald Reagan met personally with his critics. The confrontations took several forms: first, he and Mrs. Reagan invited a small group of legislators and their wives to have dinner at the governor's residence twice a week. They maintained this schedule until they had hosted every member of the Senate and the Assembly, and his wife. The evenings were kept scrupulously bi-partisan.

Dinner was elegant with candlelight and California wine. Cocktails were served by Orientals in native costume. Conversation was kept flowing by the always gracious Mrs. Reagan.* The guests

---

* Nancy Reagan is a lovely, soft-spoken woman of 43, looking years younger, who sees her primary duty as providing as normal a home as possible for her husband and their two children, Patti and Skipper. But she *is* the governor's wife and because she has poise, is intelligent and knows issues and politics, it's quite likely she will be doing more rather than less politicking in the years to come. She does not hide her deep affection for and pride in her husband: "If anything, my pride in him grows each day. He shows tremendous courage, integrity and strength. You learn an awful lot about somebody when you

were enchanted. Upon the completion of dinner, the evening took a typically Reagan turn. The governor would rise and say, "Gentlemen, let's go downstairs." There the men were confronted by a gigantic electric train set covering nearly one half of a large recreation room, an upright piano and a pool table. Taking off his tux, the governor would run the trains while a senator would strike up a tune on the piano and an assemblyman would send a cue ball hurtling into the racked balls.

After such an evening, it was difficult for legislators to describe Ronald Reagan as an extremist or know-nothing. In fact, several began to admit that they *liked* him.

The other part of the campaign was and is a series of two breakfasts a week with legislators. No holds are barred during these bi-partisan meetings as governor and assemblyman or senator talk about a bill, a speech or just politics.

Finally, a rule was adopted and adhered to that any legislator can see the governor within 24 hours of making the request.

By the end of the first session, the legislature had passed both his budget and tax program as well as a major part of his anti-crime program. He won a partial victory on his campaign promise to reduce property taxes by directing $148 million in state funds to local school boards. His bills to encourage water reclamation and governmental reorganization were passed. In the opinion of pollster Don Muchmore, the governor did so well

---

see them in difficult situations, as to how they handle themselves and on what level they choose to make their stands.

"Ronnie has always stuck to his principles and has never gotten personal or vindictive. If your position is strong, you don't have to indulge in that kind of thing."

that "by Californians' judgment, Reagan's presidential possibilities are considerably improved." Reporter Julius Duscha of the Washington *Post* wrote: "Reagan demonstrated during the seven-month legislative session that he has what it takes to be effective in dealing with a legislative body."

As he had promised, the governor went directly to the people to explain why his budget was so big, describe the economies which would have to be made, and tell why, despite all these efforts, it would be necessary to raise taxes—at least this year.

In a televised "Report to the People" on July 9, Governor Reagan stated that "California state government, like Topsy, in recent years has grown—with no real effort to control or direct that growth." He said that although the State Constitution requires that the budget be balanced "we found this was not the case." He mentioned, as he had before, that spending had been exceeding revenues by more than a million dollars a day—a $386 million annual deficit.

Reagan pointed out that the Brown administration had borrowed $194 million from trust funds—which had to be repaid out of new taxes. He regretfully reported that despite all possible economies the 1967-68 budget would still total just under $5.1 billion—"the biggest budget in our state's history."

It would be necessary, he said, to raise taxes by $937 million to balance the budget and pay old debts. The tax raise, he admitted, was also a new record.

But the governor stressed that the tax bill and the budget "does not represent my philosophy of government . . . . I still think the government of California costs the people of California too much."

He mentioned twice the group of business and professional experts who were voluntarily studying the state government. He reported that their recommendations on tax reform and governmental economies would be presented in late fall or winter. By that time, he said, "we will have a pretty good idea of what government should cost and how big it should be and taxes will be geared to real need and not to some empire-building concept of government growing bigger and bigger just for the sake of growing."

His ending was characteristically candid:

"Remember, this is not the government's state, this is the people's state and the people's government. You can have sound financial policies, you can have solid state programs and you can have fair and equitable taxes *if* you demand them loud and clear."

In this "Report" and at every other opportunity, Reagan emphasized that the job could not be accomplished overnight. Curiously, both ultra-liberal and ultra-conservative critics have accused the governor of "selling out" his conservative principles. Commented a *New Republic* reporter, "Ronald Reagan turns out to be a kind of Hubert Humphrey of the right" (a reference to the Vice President's support of the war in Vietnam—a position no "decent," self-respecting liberal could possibly take). An ultra-conservative legislator from Southern California called the governor's budget and tax program, "A tragic end to the brightest hope on the American political scene today."

But most Californians are willing to practice

more patience. They haven't forgotten what Ronald Reagan told a reporter in the middle of his budget-tax struggle:

"Over and over again in the campaign I called attention to the people that things had been on a toboggan and it couldn't be reversed all at once. . . . I think there are some people—a few—who would want me to jump off a cliff with a flag flying. But the bulk of the response I am getting is that people realize I am trying to do everything I promised in the campaign."

The polls confirmed his assessment. On July 11, Mervin Field's California Poll reported that 74% of California's voters credited Governor Reagan with doing a fair or good job. The findings represented an *advance* of 8% over the preceding month. Only 17% of the people thought he was doing a poor job. Field stated that the 17% poor rating was the lowest for any governor in 20 years.

After seven months in office, Governor Reagan was sticking to his philosophical guns and scoring direct hits with the people—and the communications media.

The *Wall Street Journal* headlined: "His Performance Is Getting Generally High Marks."

A reporter from the liberal British newspaper, the *Observer*, wrote: "It is also clear that Reagan himself . . . is no nut: that he is, indeed, shrewd, a quick learner, and a reconciler rather than a hater."

Columnist Roscoe Drummond wrote: "He has shown that he is not afraid to tread on some toes, that he can make decisions and stand behind them, that he intends to redeem his campaign promises. He is proving in practice that the idea he is an empty-headed actor reading somebody else's script is bunk."

The San Diego *Union* editorialized: "To persons who voted for the governor and now are seeing their wishes followed, or to his loyal opposition which will benefit in spite of itself, the first 100 Reagan Days are encouraging.

"With hundreds of days more to come the task undoubtedly will get done."

The Los Angeles *Times,* commenting on the tendency of the Eastern press to underrate Reagan, understated:

"Maybe something is happening in the West that the East doesn't know about yet."

What is that "something"?

Conservative columnist Thomas Lane wondered whether Reagan can lead a national political renaissance and answered his own question: "If he retains the confidence of the people of California in his renaissance of freedom and progress, he may in 1968 be the only candidate with demonstrated qualifications for restoring integrity to the Federal government."

Walter Scratch, political editor of the Santa Monica *Outlook,* wrote: "Governments, down through the ages, have induced people to look to them instead of to themselves for their needs. If Reagan's philosophy prevails, despite the opposition it will get from the forces of materialism, it will help us to rely upon the unlimited resources within each of us instead of relying upon government for our needs."

And Governor Reagan told a rapt audience in Los Angeles: "If we succeed here, if we show we can build a creative society at the state level, we can start a prairie fire that will sweep this country clean of big brother government and again permit government of and by the people to grow and flourish.

"Our goal is as it has always been—freedom—and whatever the price, it's less than the cost of doing without it."

Will he succeed? It is far too early to make any final judgment, but the first months of the Creative Society suggest strongly that government of, by and for the people is possible if the man at the top is intelligent enough, determined enough and persuasive enough and if he can bring forth those same qualities in the people he represents.

As Ronald Reagan has said, "This year is only the beginning." But it is a promising beginning, so promising that it appears that a former sportscaster from Tampico, Ill., by way of Des Moines, a former star in Hollywood "B" pictures, a liberal Democrat turned conservative Republican, a sometimes corny, always square citizen politician, will be successful in helping the biggest state in the union and its 20 million citizens to find the rest of themselves.

EPILOGUE

Time: August 8, 1968
Place: Convention Hall, Miami Beach, Fla.
Cast: Twenty thousand delegates, alternates, spectators and news media personnel at the 1968 GOP national convention, plus tens of millions of Americans tuned in via television and radio.
Action: The silver-tongued, silver-haired orator pauses dramatically and then brings his stirring speech to a familiar close: "And so, my fellow Republicans and my fellow Americans, it is my great honor and high privilege to give you the next president of the United States—the Honorable Ronald Reagan of California!"

Bedlam ensues as Governor Reagan steps onto the platform to accept the Republican nomination for president.

A midsummer night's dream? Or nightmare for an Eastern liberal? It may not be a dream at all for Ronald Reagan has emerged after less than one year in office as one of the most popular Republicans in the country and a not so long-shot for his party's nomination for president in 1968.

George Gallup corroborated this conclusion on Aug. 2, 1967, by releasing the results of a "trial heat" between President Johnson and Governor Reagan:

Johnson	51%
Reagan	39%
Undecided	10%

Commented Gallup, with typical scientific restraint: "For a man who has held political office barely six months, (Reagan's) showing must be regarded as impressive." Reagan supporters were prone to use stronger adjectives like "sensational" and "phenomenal." It's difficult to blame them. Earlier surveys showed Johnson with a 51-43 lead over Nixon and a 49-44 margin over Romney—adding up to a near tie among Reagan, Nixon and Romney.

Furthermore, Reagan ran *even* with Johnson among independents, an all-important voting group for a Republican, who cannot depend upon his own party to provide him with enough votes. The results by party affiliation:

	Rep.	Dem.	Ind.
Reagan	74%	14%	44%
Johnson	19	76	44
Undecided	7	10	12

The reverberations of the poll, it was thought, would echo for months to come. Hardly less shocking was the victory of Republican Milton Marks of San Francisco in a special election on Aug. 15 which, in effect, gave the GOP control of the California State Senate. Marks overcame a 2-1 Democratic registration to win a Senate vacancy that threw the upper house into a 20-20 party standoff. However, in the event of a tie, Republican Lt. Gov. Robert Finch will vote to break the deadlock. Marks beat ultra-liberal John Burton, a Democratic assemblyman, who spent almost all of his time attacking Reagan. The Marks victory was interpreted everywhere as a major political triumph for Governor Reagan. San Francisco was the only major city in California to vote heavily for Pat Brown in 1966. Marks' win made California Reaganland from top to bottom.

The man from California was benefitting from his long career in films and television and as the result of his successful 1967 trips to the East and Midwest, the attention focused on his administration in Sacramento and, perhaps most importantly of all, a television appearance with Senator Robert Kennedy on CBS' "Town Meeting of the World" on Monday night, May 15. The program was designed to be a bi-partisan discussion of America's image with Reagan and Kennedy supplying the answers to questions posed by a group of London-based foreign students. But the students were so aggressively hostile toward the United States, particularly its Vietnam policy, that the hour-long show evolved into a sharp debate. Who came out on top? *Newsweek* concluded: "It was political rookie Reagan who left old campaigner Kennedy blinking when the session ended."

The New York Senator was consistently on the defensive and obviously uncomfortable while attempting to explain the war in Vietnam. Reagan, in contrast, *willingly* explained why the U.S. was in Vietnam, challenged correctly misleading statistics which several of the students used and emphasized the traditional American quest for peace. When a coldly contemptuous student rattled off a set speech about U.S. aggression, Reagan reminded him that after World War II the U.S. possessed unrivaled power, including the atomic bomb, but did not try to impose its will upon the world.

"Can you honestly say in your heart," he asked, "that had the Soviet Union been in a comparable position with that bomb, or today's Red Chinese . . . that the world would not today have been conquered by that force?"

A hypothetical question, mumbled the student, lapsing into silence.

At the program's end, although the moderator had stated that there would be no closing remarks, Kennedy interrupted him to make an obviously rehearsed short speech, including a quotation from Plato. Reagan calmly topped the bushy-haired Senator with the following advice to the students in London and everywhere:

"I think that you should weigh everything that is proposed to you—everything in the line of government, law, and economic theory—but weigh it on this one scale: that it should never at any time offer you some kind of sanctuary or security in exchange for your right to fly as high and as far as your own strength and ability will take you as an individual, with no ceiling put on that effort . . . . Always reserve the right for yourself to be free."

Commented the television critic of the San Francisco *Chronicle*, which had endorsed Pat Brown:

"He was the first to volunteer answers to the difficult questions of America's violation of the Geneva agreement and on the Diem regime in Vietnam, and his grasp of the facts in the international area was impressive. The success of this performance against sizable odds can be considered a major step in his career."

Quite suddenly, everyone was talking about Ronald Reagan and the presidency.

Pat Brown declared that "beyond peradventure" Reagan was running for the office of president. A *Newsweek* cover story about the California governor included an insert that was headlined: "The GOP View of '68: Why Reagan and Percy May Be Fighting It Out." The magazine offered this analysis of Reagan:

"His style is an amalgam of Dwight Eisenhower's lofty superiority to petty partisanship (and sometimes his garbled syntax), George Romney's infectious piety, Barry Goldwater's evangelistic faith in the conservative credo—and, most of all, Reagan's own unmatched ability to convince people that the honest face they see on their TV screens is an accurate reflection of the inner man."

At the other end of the continent, Gov. Nelson Rockefeller of New York said that although he did not agree with many of his stands, Reagan had showed "plenty of guts" in his budget-tax fight. A few balloons have even been lofted about a Rockefeller-Reagan ticket—although the New York governor insists stoutly that George Romney is his man.

Many combinations have been and will undoubtedly be suggested between now and the GOP convention, but one of the most intriguing is Ronald Reagan and Senator Edward Brooke of Massachusetts, a Negro. *Newsweek* reported in late June, "Some professional Democrats now say privately that the strongest team the GOP can field in '68 is one headed by Ronald Reagan and Edward Brooke." *Newsweek* did not mention that a Reagan-Brooke ticket was first suggested by the noted Negro journalist and prominent conservative, George Schuyler. In a column published on January 6, Schuyler wrote:

"Reagan and Brooke would be an ideal pair to head the Republican ticket in 1968." The writer said that Reagan's conservatism and voter appeal combined with Brooke's proven ability and attraction to liberal and uncommitted voters could solve the old GOP dilemma: "How to win back support from city Negroes, union members, and the growing number of the uncommitted, and, at the same time, hold on to the conservative elements that have supported them in the recent past?"

The California governor did not go unnoticed overseas. *Pravda,* the Soviet Communist Party newspaper, printed a satirical cartoon of Reagan with the caption: "On a white horse to the White House—this is how Americans view the plans of the dashing horseman."

The New York *Times* exercised its usual moderation in an editorial which followed Reagan's wildly applauded appearance before 1500 delegates and guests at the Young Republican National Federation convention in June:

"If Mr. Goldwater was unpersuasive in the role of a future President, Mr. Reagan is downright implausible . . . .

"But his appeal to the young is readily understandable. In politics, the characteristic attitude of young people is not liberal or radical, conservative or reactionary. Rather, it is militant, uncompromising, emotional . . . .

"Governor Reagan, who politically was only born yesterday, is naturally at home with the fanatical young Republicans despite his comparatively advanced age. But the wise men of the Republican party had best emulate their party symbol, the elephant, and never forget the lessons of 1964 . . . ."

Several unlikely Republicans disagreed with this estimate of Reagan, including Gov. Tom McCall of Oregon, a supporter of Nelson Rockefeller for the presidential nomination. Said McCall: "Reagan is the best drawing card in either party, the hottest political property the Republican Party has. He has more going for him than any other governor today."

Gov. Paul Laxalt of Nevada labeled Reagan a "major contender" for the nomination.

Senator George Murphy of California stated: "If he should turn out to be one of the best governors, I don't think there would be any way in the world that he could stop the people at the convention supporting him."

And on May 26, Senator Thomas Kuchel finally admitted that Reagan was here to stay by endorsing the governor's decision to enter California's presidential primary in 1968 as a "favorite son" candidate. Kuchel added that Reagan was "one of several potential candidates who must be considered" at the national convention.

Conceded Charles Warren, California's Democratic chairman: "A year ago we were laughing Ronnie Reagan off as governor. Now we're not laughing him off as president, and as things are, he would win in California."

The ultra-liberal Ripon Society, a very small but widely-publicized organization addicted to giving unheeded advice to the GOP, wasn't laughing either, commenting in its monthly publication: "Ronald Reagan's Presidential ambitions must be taken seriously, not because they are justified by the candidate's own experience or by his vision for America, but because he threatens by the same combination of organizational maneuvering and narrowly based programs to make 1968 another year of disaster and disunity for the Republican party."

But one man's disaster is another's delight. From Palm Springs, in March, Dwight Eisenhower said: "There are a number of men who would make fine presidents in our party, and Reagan is one of the men I admire most in the world. . . . No one knows what is in the future, but when duty calls he has to answer."

House Republican leader Gerald Ford said that Reagan is "certainly a qualified person for higher office."

Congressman Mel Laird, chairman of the House Republican Conference, has stated that "Governor Reagan is obviously doing an outstanding job as governor of California" and praised him for "his forthrightness and willingness to face up to hard decisions."

In a letter to this writer, Richard Nixon said:

"Governor Reagan's success as Chief Executive of California is no real surprise to those of us who have known him for a number of years. Long before he was taken seriously in politics, Ronald Reagan was a serious student of public issues and the art of government. He is a tremendously gifted man, with a willingness to work and a demonstrated capacity for learning and growth. As a candidate, of course, he has had a spectacular political career, and he must be considered a credit and an asset to the party in the nation as well as California."

No polling of Republican opinion would be complete without several candid words from Mr. Conservative, Barry Goldwater, who told me:

"I consider Governor Reagan to be the brightest dark horse of the whole stable and I would go so far as to say that if he as much as said, 'I want to be the Presidential nominee,' that he could have it almost hands down. I do not think he will say this, however, because in my heart I do not think he really wants it this go round."

With regard to the Creative Society, the Senator responded characteristically:

"Every governor dreams up some kind of title for his administration. We have had Rockefeller with his, Romney with his and now Ronnie has come up with a Creative Society. I don't think anyone pays a lot of attention to the labels; it is just a matter of getting the job done. If they like the man and he is doing his work, then I don't give a damn if they call it The Cauliflower Society, it would be popular."

Evidence of Reagan's popularity could be found everywhere. In January, 1967, George Gallup released the findings of a poll to determine the men most admired by Americans in 1966. The top ten were: Lyndon Johnson, Dwight Eisenhower, Robert Kennedy, Rev. Billy Graham, Pope Paul VI, U Thant, Everett Dirksen, George Romney, Richard Nixon, and . . . Ronald Reagan.

Reagan for President Committees have formed in several states, including Michigan where Robert M. Smith founded the very first Reagan club in Owosso on Nov. 19, *1964* (*sic*).

It has even been rumored that F. Clifton White, the major architect of Barry Goldwater's nomination campaign in 1964, will organize a draft Reagan movement in late 1967. In July, White denied the report commenting, "I don't think I would even advise Reagan at this point to get into the race."

But times change and so do the intentions of men.

Which brings us to three questions:

(1) Will Ronald Reagan run for his party's presidential nomination in 1968?

(2) Can he win the nomination?

(3) Can he beat Lyndon Johnson?

Here is the consensus, understandably conditional, of the opinions of several dozen politicians and political analysts across the country:

(1) Ronald Reagan will make a determined, organized effort to get the GOP's presidential nomination only *if* and *after* it has become clear that Richard Nixon will not win the nomination. Nixon is adjudged by the overwhelming majority of Republicans as the most qualified Republican, and perhaps American, to be in the White House. This majority would very much like to see Nixon President, based on his qualifications, his close loss in 1960 against JFK, his work for the Party down through the years, and the desire to have someone experienced in foreign affairs at the helm. But Nixon must first convince his fellow Republicans and the rest of the American public that he can still win a political race—and that means the primaries. By June 1, 1968, after New Hampshire, Wisconsin, Nebraska and Oregon, everyone will know whether Nixon can still win, or not.

Reagan has not been coy about the presidential "thing." He announced at a news conference in February, 1967, that he would be a favorite son candidate in the California primary in 1968. He explained that his candidacy was designed to "keep the glue on the recently healed wound" of his party, resulting from the bitter Goldwater-Rockefeller primary in 1964. He added that he did not expect to be the GOP standard bearer. Everything he has said since has been consistent with his initial statements. He will allow his name to be entered in the Oregon, Wisconsin and Nebraska primaries (but not New Hampshire) because he could only remove his name if he stated he "is not and does not intend to become" a candidate.

Reagan has explained that it would be "presumptuous" for him to make a Sherman-like statement.* He has also said: "If the Republican party comes beating at my door, I wouldn't say, 'Get lost, fellows,' but that isn't going to happen." He feels that it would be "inconsistent" to be a favorite son in California but refuse to be on the ballot in Oregon and the other states. But he has emphasized that he will not campaign in any state. Whatever his personal feelings, Governor Reagan is proud and aware of California's position as the nation's most populous state. As the Sacramento *Union*'s political writer asked: "What's *wrong* with a Californian being considered Presidential timber?"

(2) Ronald Reagan can win the nomination. It must be added that Romney, Nixon, Nelson Rockefeller and Sen. Charles Percy can also win, depending upon the primaries, favorite son inclinations, external events, etc. Part of the proof lies in an April, 1967 Gallup Poll about the preferences of Republican county chairmen regarding 1968. County chairmen are local party leaders who have an important part in selecting convention delegates; in fact, many *are* delegates. They are conservative, for the most part, and have been largely responsible for selecting the party's nominee at every convention in recent years except in

* Approached about running for the presidency, Civil War General William Tecumseh Sherman replied: "If nominated I will not run, and if elected I will not serve."

1952. Then the majority were for Senator Robert Taft, who, of course, lost the nomination to General Dwight D. Eisenhower.

Gallup asked 3,300 GOP county or town chairmen whom they personally preferred as the Republican candidate for President in 1968. The top five:

Richard Nixon	1,227
George Romney	341
Ronald Reagan	233
Charles Percy	119
Nelson Rockefeller	67

When asked to choose between Nixon and Romney, they replied:

Nixon 1,562   Romney 523   Undecided 52

They were also asked to give their second choices, and when the votes for Nixon were redistributed on the basis of second choices, the bulk went to Reagan, with the following results:

Reagan	429
Romney	249
Percy	160
James Rhodes	84

In addition, without any alarums or flourishes, Reagan supporters have moved into key party positions at every level: Reagan sits on the executive committee of the Republican Governor's Association; Senator Murphy of California is chairman of the Republican Senatorial Campaign Committee; Congressman Bob Wilson of California is chairman of the Republican Congressional Campaign Committee; Gladys O'Donnell of California is president of the National Federation of

EPILOGUE

Republican Women; and Jack McDonald of Tennessee, new chairman of the Young Republicans, is a staunch conservative. The women's federation and the YR's are the two main volunteer organizations which provide the GOP with man- and woman-power.

If Reagan should launch a run for the nomination, he would need a sizeable sum of money—something like $1 million for the period between June 1 and August 10 when the national convention would end. With such men as Henry Salvatori in California, Gordon Reed in Connecticut and other wealthy conservatives in Texas, Pennsylvania and across the country, the money could certainly be raised.

With funds, a political base and voter appeal, Reagan would lack only a solid national organization to win the nomination. One could become available. Nixon himself has stated that if he does not win "X" number of primaries, he will not belabor the point; he will withdraw. In that event, it is entirely logical that the Nixon organization would transfer allegiance and operations to nominating Ronald Reagan.

3) This is the most speculative of all three questions: Can Ronald Reagan defeat President Lyndon Johnson? This book is being written in the summer of 1967—almost a year before the GOP convention and 15 months before Election Day, 1968. *Anything* can happen in politics, and usually does.

The polls showed Nixon far ahead of John F. Kennedy when their presidential struggle began in September, 1960, but following only one national telecast, the first of the Great Debates, Kennedy surged into the lead, lost some ground, was counted an almost certain winner in late October and won by only 118,550 votes out of 68 million cast.

In 1964, Johnson was never seriously troubled by Barry Goldwater until the Walter Jenkins episode in mid-October threw the Democrats into a panic. The unexpected happened. Goldwater had been banging away at the issues of corruption and immorality in government for months and suddenly one of the President's closest aides, a man who sat in on meetings of the National Security Council, was revealed to be a homosexual. It is possible that millions of votes might have shifted. It is possible that Johnson might have mishandled the incident, lost his temper, struck back at Goldwater in some wild, unreasoned political fashion, thereby shifting more millions of votes. But then lightning struck two, three, four times. Within 48 hours of the exposé of Walter Jenkins, Khrushchev was deposed, the Chinese Communists set off an atomic bomb and the British elections resulted in a change of government. The Jenkins story went from page one to page thirty-four in one day.

Who can foretell, therefore, what might happen in the next year? Ho Chi Minh might sue for peace. Stokely Carmichael might admit membership in the Communist party, or enter a monastery. A tax raise might cool off the threat of inflation. Labor might not call all the strikes it is threatening it will call. Americans for Democratic Action might forgive LBJ. The President might work his special brand of political legerdemain on the many serious problems confronting the nation.

But right now, this year, the American public is dissatisfied, worried, bewildered, even frightened. America no longer seems to be the Garden of

Eden. Chaos reigns as the King of a year-long Mardi Gras fueled by pot, LSD and Molotov cocktails. The people are in a mood to try anything, listen to anybody who seems to have the answer, *any* answer to restore sanity and stability to a spinning, swirling world.

Johnson, confronted by a Ronald Reagan, could unleash hundreds of barbs about his inexperience, his acting, his make-up, his Borax commercials, his conservatism, his liberalism, as Pat Brown did, but he would also be obliged to answer the charge that he, Lyndon Baines Johnson, is not getting the job done, and it's time for a change. As they say, *Ya Basta?*

In one sense, Johnson versus Reagan would be a national replay of Brown versus Reagan in 1966—the old pro pitted against the tyro. In another sense, Johnson versus Reagan would be a repeat of 1960—but with the party roles reversed. Johnson would be playing Nixon, on the defensive, explaining the record of the incumbent administration, concerned about his "image," looking older, tired, wrinkled, while Reagan would be playing Kennedy, youthful, confident, handsome, smiling, letting go a rat-a-tat-tat of figures and statistics, trying to get the country moving forward again, asking people to help themselves and their country.

One final question remains to be asked: What *kind* of a president would Ronald Reagan make?

I have attempted to give as complete an account as possible of the man's family, his childhood, his education, his work, his friends, his interests, his victories, his defeats, his hopes, his fears, his dreams and his ambitions. I have tried to show how he reacted when the going was difficult, when he was challenged, when he was frustrated, when he was stopped or knocked down. It is my hope that you now understand Ronald Reagan well enough to have a good notion of how he would conduct himself in almost any situation, including the presidency.

In the final analysis, the question of what kind of President Reagan would make rests in turn on four other questions: (1) Would he appoint sound, experienced people as his personal assistants and as the heads of the various Federal departments and agencies? (2) Would he work with both aisles of both Houses to make the best possible decisions for the general good? (3) Would he conduct our foreign policy with firmness and restraint? (4) Would he get more out of the American public by communicating the need for sacrifice, hard work, and mutual assistance? In other words, would he be able to do in Washington what he is presently doing in Sacramento ?

For those who say, "That kind of national government is impossible today," and "How *dare* he even consider the presidency in view of his lack of experience," I offer Ronald Reagan's own answer:

"I ran for governor without experience. Sometimes it helps—you don't know what you can't do."

APPENDIX

THE SPEECH
(Delivered over national television by Ronald Reagan on Oct. 27, 1964.)

I am going to talk of controversial things. I make no apology for this. I have been talking on this subject for ten years, obviously under the administration of both parties. I mention this only because it seems impossible to legitimately debate the issues of the day without being subjected to name-calling and the application of labels. Those who deplore use of the terms "pink" and "leftist" are themselves guilty of branding all who oppose their liberalism as right wing extremists. How long can we afford the luxury of this family fight when we are at war with the most dangerous enemy ever known to man?

If we lose that war, and in so doing lose our freedom, it has been said history will record with the greatest astonishment that those who had the most to lose did the least to prevent its happening. The guns are silent in this war but frontiers fall while those who should be warriors prefer neutrality. Not too long ago two friends of mine were talking to a Cuban refugee. He was a business man who had escaped from Castro. In the midst of his tale of horrible experiences, one of my friends turned to the other and said, "We don't know how lucky we are." The Cuban stopped and said, "How lucky you are? *I* had some place to escape to." And in that sentence he told the entire story. If freedom is lost here there is no place to escape to.

It's time we asked ourselves if we still know the freedoms intended for us by the Founding Fathers. James Madison said, "We base all our experiments on the capacity of mankind for self-government." This idea that government was beholden to the people, that it had no other source of power except the sovereign people, is still the newest, most unique idea in all the long history of man's relation to man. For almost two centuries we have proved man's capacity for self-government, but today we are told we must choose between a left and right or, as others suggest, a third alternative, a kind of safe middle ground. I suggest to you there is no left or right, only an up or down. Up to the maximum of individual freedom consistent with law and order, or down to the ant heap of totalitarianism, and regardless of their humanitarian purpose those who would sacrifice freedom for security have, whether they know it or not, chosen this downward path. Plutarch warned, "The real destroyer of the liberties of the people is he who spreads among them bounties, donations and benefits."

Today there is an increasing number who can't see a fat man standing beside a thin one without automatically coming to the conclusion the fat man got that way by taking advantage of the thin one. So they would seek the answer to all the problems of human need through government. Howard K. Smith of television fame has written, "The profit motive is outmoded. It must be replaced by the incentives of the welfare state." He says, "The distribution of goods must be effected by a planned economy."

Another articulate spokesman for the welfare state defines liberalism as meeting the material needs of the masses through the full power of centralized government. I for one find it disturbing when a representative refers to the free men and women of this country as the masses, but beyond this the full power of centralized government was the very thing the Founding Fathers sought to minimize. They knew you don't control things, you can't control the economy without controlling *people*. So we have come to a time for choosing. Either we accept the responsibility for our own destiny, or we abandon the American Revolution and confess that an intellectual belief in a far-distant capitol can plan our lives for us better than we can plan them ourselves.

Already the hour is late. Government has laid its hand on health, housing, farming, industry, commerce, education, and to an ever increasing degree interferes with the people's right to know. Government tends to grow, government programs take on weight and momentum as public servants say, always with the best of intentions, "What greater service we could render if only we had a little more money and a little more power." But the truth is that outside of its legitimate function, government does nothing as well or as economically as the private sector of the economy. What better example do we have of this than government's involvement in the farm economy over the last 30 years. One-fourth of farming has seen a steady decline in the per capita consumption of everything it produces. That one-fourth is regulated and subsidized by government.

In contrast, the three-fourths of farming unregulated and unsubsidized has seen a 21 per cent increase in the per capita consumption of all its produce. Since 1955 the cost of the farm program has nearly doubled. Direct payment to farmer is eight times as great as it was nine years ago, but farm income remains unchanged while farm surplus is bigger. In that same period we have seen a decline of five million in the farm population, but an increase in the number of Department of Agriculture employees.

There is now one such employee for every 30 farms in the United States, and still they can't figure how 66 shiploads of grain headed for Austria could disappear without a trace, and Billy Sol Estes never left shore. Three years ago the government put into effect a program to curb the over-production of feed grain. Now, two and a half billion dollars later, the corn crop is 100 million bushels bigger than before the program started. And the cost of the program prorates out to $43 for every dollar bushel of corn we don't grow. Nor is this the only example of the price we pay for government meddling. Some government programs with the passage of time take on a sacrosanct quality.

One such considered above criticism, sacred as motherhood, is TVA. This program started as a flood control project; the Tennessee Valley was periodically ravaged by destructive floods. The Army Engineers set out to solve this problem. They said that it was possible that once in 500 years there could be a total capacity flood that would inundate some 600,000 acres. Well the Engineers fixed that. They made a permanent lake which inundated a million acres. This solved the problem of the floods, but the annual interest on the TVA debt is five times as great as the annual flood damage they sought to correct.

Of course, you will point out that TVA gets electric power from the impounded waters, and this is true, but today 85 per cent of TVA's electricity is generated in coal burning steam plants. Now perhaps you'll charge that I'm overlooking the navigable waterway that was created, providing cheap barge traffic, but the bulk of the freight barged on that waterway is coal being shipped to the TVA steam plants, and the cost of maintaining that channel each year would pay for shipping all of the coal by rail, and there would be money left over.

One last argument remains: The prosperity produced by such large programs of government spending. Certainly there are few areas where more spending has taken place. The Labor Department lists 50 per cent of the 169 counties in the Tennessee Valley as permanent areas of poverty, distress, and unemployment.

Meanwhile, back in the city, under Urban Renewal, the assault on freedom carries on. Private property rights have become so diluted that public interest is anything a few planners decide it should be. In Cleveland, Ohio, to get a project under way, city officials reclassified 84 buildings as substandard in spite of the fact their own inspectors had previously pronounced these buildings sound. The owners stood by and watched 26 million dollars worth of property as it was destroyed by the headache ball. Senate Bill 628 says, "Any property, be it home or commercial structure, can be declared slum or blighted and the owner has no recourse at law. The Law Division of the Library of Congress and the General Accounting Office have said that the Courts will have to rule against the owner."

HOUSING. In one key Eastern city a man owning a blighted area sold his property to Urban Renewal for several million dollars. At the same time, he submitted his own plan for the rebuilding of this area and the government sold him back his own property for 22 per cent of what they paid. Now the government announces, "We are going to build subsidized housing in the thousands where we have been building in the hundreds." At the same time FHA and the Veterans Administration reveal they are holding 120 thousand housing units reclaimed from mortgage foreclosure, mostly because the low down payment, and the easy terms brought the owners to a point where they realized the unpaid balance on the homes amounted to a sum greater than the homes were worth, so they just walked out the front door, possibly to take up residence in newer subsidized housing, again with little or no down payment and easy terms.

Some of the foreclosed homes have already been bulldozed into the earth, others, it has been announced, will be refurbished and put on sale for down payments as low as $100 and 35 years to pay. This will give the bulldozers a second crack. It is in the area of social welfare that government has found its most fertile growing bed. So many of us accept our responsibility for those less fortunate. We are susceptible to humanitarian appeals.

Federal welfare spending is today ten times greater than it was in the dark depths of the depression. Federal, state, and local welfare combined spend 45 billion dollars a year. Now the government has announced that 20 per cent, some 9.3 million families, are poverty stricken on the basis that they have less than a $3,000 a year income.

If this present welfare spending was prorated equally among these poverty stricken families, we could give each family more than $4,500 a year. Actually, direct aid to the poor averages less than $600 per family. There must be some administrative overhead somewhere. Now, are we to believe that another billion dollar program added to the half a hundred programs and the 45 billion dollars, will, through some magic, end poverty? For three decades we have tried to solve unemployment by government planning, without success. The more the plans fail, the more the planners plan.

The latest is the Area Redevelopment Agency, and in two years less than one-half of one per cent of the unemployed could attribute new jobs to this agency, and the cost to the taxpayer for each job found was $5,000. But beyond the great bureaucratic waste, what are we doing to the people we seek to help?

Recently a judge told me of an incident in his court. A fairly young woman with six children, pregnant with her seventh, came to him for a divorce. Under his questioning it became apparent her husband did not share this desire. Then the whole story came out. Her husband was a laborer earning $250 a month. By divorcing him she could get an $80 raise. She was eligible for $350 a month from the Aid to Dependent Children Program. She had been talked into the divorce by two friends who had already done this very thing. But any time we question the schemes of the do-gooders, we are denounced as being opposed to their humanitarian goal. It seems impossible to legitimately debate their solutions with the assumption that all of us share the desire to help those less fortunate. They tell us we are always against, never for anything. Well, it isn't so much that Liberals are ignorant. It's just that they know so much that isn't so.

We are for a provision that destitution should not follow unemployment by reason of old age. For that reason we have accepted Social Security as a step toward meeting that problem. However, we are against the irresponsibility of those who charge that any criticism or suggested improvement of the program means we want to end payment to those who depend on Social Security for a livelihood.

FISCAL IRRESPONSIBILITY. We have been told in millions of pieces of literature and press releases that Social Security is an insurance program, but the executives of Social Security appeared before the Supreme Court in the case of *Nestor v. Fleming* and proved to the Court's satisfaction that it is not insurance but is a welfare program, and Social Security dues are a tax for the general use of the government. Well it can't be both, insurance and welfare. Later appearing before a Congressional Committee they admitted that Social Security is today 298 billion dollars in the red. This fiscal irresponsibility has already caught up with us.

Faced with a bankruptcy we find that today a young man in his early twenties, going to work at less than an average salary, will with his employer pay into Social Security an amount which could provide the young man with a retirement insurance policy guaranteeing $220 a month at age 65, and the government promises him $127.

Now, are we so lacking in business sense that we cannot put this program on a sound actuarial basis, so that those who do depend on it won't come to the cupboard and find it bare, and at the same time can't we introduce voluntary features so that those who can make better provision for themselves are allowed to do so? Incidentally, we might also allow participants in Social Security to name their own beneficiaries, which they cannot do in the present program. These are not insurmountable problems.

YOUTH AID PLANS. We have today 30 million workers protected by industrial and union pension funds that are soundly financed by some 70 billion dollars invested in corporate securities and income earning real estate. I think we are for telling our senior citizens that no one in this country should be denied medical care for lack of funds but we are against forcing all citizens into a compulsory government program regardless of need. Now the government has turned its attention to our young people, and suggests that it can solve the problem of school dropouts and juvenile delinquency through some kind of revival of the old C.C.C. camps. The suggested plan prorates out to a cost of $4,700 a year for each young person we want to help. We can send them to Harvard for $2,700 a year. Of course, don't get me wrong—I'm not suggesting Harvard as the answer to juvenile delinquency.

We are for an international organization where the nations of the world can legitimately seek peace. We are against subordinating American interests to an organization so structurally unsound that a two-thirds majority can be mustered in the U.N. General Assembly among nations representing less than 10 per cent of the world population.

Is there not something of hypocrisy in assailing our allies for so-called vestiges of colonialism while we engage in a conspiracy of silence about the peoples enslaved by the

APPENDIX

Soviet in the satellite nations? We are for aiding our allies by sharing our material blessings with those nations which share our fundamental beliefs. We are against doling out money, government to government, which ends up financing socialism all over the world.

We set out to help 19 war ravaged countries at the end of World War II. We are now helping 107. We have spent 146 billion dollars. Some of that money bought a $2 million yacht for Haile Selassie. We bought dress suits for Greek undertakers. We bought 1,000 TV sets, with 23-inch screens, for a country where there is no electricity, and some of our foreign aid funds provided extra wives for Kenya government officials. When Congress moved to cut foreign aid they were told that if they cut it one dollar they endangered national security, and then Senator Harry Byrd revealed that since its inception foreign aid has rarely spent its allotted budget. It has today $21 billion in unexpended funds.

Some time ago Dr. Howard Kershner was speaking to the prime minister of Lebanon. The prime minister told him proudly that his little country balanced its budget each year. It had no public debt, no inflation, a modest tax rate and had increased its gold holdings from 70 to 120 million dollars. When he finished, Dr. Kershner said, "Mr. Prime Minister, my country hasn't balanced its budget 28 out of the last 40 years. My country's debt is greater than the combined debt of all the nations of the world. We have inflation, we have a tax rate that takes from the private sector a percentage of income greater than any civilized nation has ever taken and survived. We have lost gold at such a rate that the solvency of our currency is in danger. Do you think that my country should continue to give your country millions of dollars each year?" The prime minister smiled and said, "No, but if you are foolish enough to do it, we are going to keep on taking the money."

9 STALLS FOR 1 BULL. And so we built a model stock farm in Lebanon, and we built nine stalls for each bull. I find something peculiarly appropriate in that. We have in our vaults $15 billion in gold. We don't own an ounce. Foreign dollar claims against that gold total $27 billion. In the last six years, 52 nations have bought $7 billion worth of our gold and all 52 are receiving foreign aid.

Because no government ever voluntarily reduces itself in size, government programs once launched never go out of existence. A government agency is the nearest thing to eternal life we'll ever see on this earth. The United States Manual takes 25 pages to list by name every Congressman and Senator, and all the agencies controlled by Congress.

It then lists the agencies coming under the Executive Branch, and this requires 520 pages.

Since the beginning of the century our gross national product has increased by 33 times. In the same period the cost of Federal government has increased 234 times, and while the work force is only 1½ times greater, Federal employees number nine times as many. There are now 2½ million Federal employees. No one knows what they all do. One Congressman found out what one of them does. This man sits at a desk in Washington. Documents come to him each morning. He reads them, initials them, and passes them on to the proper agency. One day a document arrived he wasn't supposed to read, but he read it, initialled it and passed it on. Twenty-four hours later it arrived back at his desk with a memo attached that said, "You weren't supposed to read this. Erase your initials, and initial the erasure."

While the Federal government is the great offender, the idea filters down. During a period in California when our population has increased 90 per cent, the cost of state government has gone up 862 per cent and the number of employees 500 per cent. Governments, state and local, now employ one out of six of the nation's work force. If the rate of increase of the last three years continues, by 1970 one-fourth of the total work force will be employed by government. Already we have a permanent structure so big and complex it is virtually beyond the control of Congress and the comprehension of the people, and tyranny inevitably follows when this permanent structure usurps the policy-making function that belongs to elected officials.

One example of this occurred when Congress was debating whether to lend the United Nations $100 million. While they debated the State Department gave the United Nations $217 million and the United Nations used part of that money to pay the delinquent dues of Castro's Cuba.

Under bureaucratic regulations adopted with no regard to the wish of the people, we have lost much of our Constitutional freedom. For example, federal agents can invade a man's property without a warrant, can impose a fine without a formal hearing, let alone a trial by jury, and can seize and sell his property at auction to enforce payment of that fine.

RIGHTS BY DISPENSATION. An Ohio deputy fire marshal sentenced a man to prison after a secret proceeding in which the accused was not allowed to have a lawyer present. The Supreme Court upheld that sentence, ruling that it was an administrative investigation of incidents damaging to the economy. Someplace a perversion has taken place. Our natural unalienable rights are now presumed to be a dispensation of government, divisible by a vote of the majority. The greatest good for the greatest number is a high-sounding phrase but contrary to the very basis of our Nation, unless it is accompanied by recognition that we have certain rights which cannot be infringed upon, even if the individual stands outvoted by all of his fellow citizens. Without this recognition, majority rule is nothing more than mob rule.

It is time we realized that socialism can come without overt seizure of property or nationalization of private business. It matters little that you hold the title to your property or business if government can dictate policy and procedure and holds life and death power over your business. The machinery of this power already exists. Lowell Mason, former anti-trust law enforcer for the Federal Trade Commission, has written "American business is being harassed, bled and even black-jacked under a preposterous crazy quilt system of laws." There are so many that the government literally can find some charge to bring against any concern it chooses to prosecute. Are we safe in our books and records?

The natural gas producers have just been handed a 428-page questionnaire by the Federal Power Commission. It weighs ten pounds. One firm has estimated it will take 70,000 accountant man hours to fill out this questionnaire, and it must be done in quadruplicate. The Power Commission says it must have it to determine whether a proper price is being charged for gas. The National Labor Relations Board ruled that a business firm could not discontinue its shipping department even though it was more efficient and economical to subcontract this work out.

The Supreme Court has ruled the government has the right to tell a citizen what he can grow on his own land for his own use. The Secretary of Agriculture has asked for the right to imprison farmers who violate their planting quotas. One business firm has been informed by the Internal Revenue Service that it cannot take a tax deduction for its institutional advertising because this advertising espoused views not in the public interest.

A child's prayer in a school cafeteria endangers religious freedom, but the people of the Amish religion in the State of Ohio who cannot participate in Social Security because of their religious beliefs have had their livestock seized and sold at auction to enforce payment of Social Security dues.

We approach a point of no return when government becomes so huge and entrenched that we fear the consequences of upheaval and just go along with it. The Federal government accounts for one-fifth of the industrial capacity of the nation, one-fourth of all construction, holds or guarantees one-third of all mortgages, owns one-third of the land, and engages in some nineteen thousand businesses covering half a hundred different lines. The Defense Department runs 269 supermarkets. They do a gross business of $730 million a year, and lose $150 million. The government spends $11 million an hour every hour of the 24 and pretends we had a tax cut while it pursues a policy of planned inflation that will more than wipe out any benefit with depreciation of our purchasing power.

We need true tax reform that will at least make a start toward restoring for our children the American dream that wealth is denied to no one, that each individual has the right to fly as high as his strength and ability will take him. The economist Sumner Schlicter has said, "If a visitor from Mars looked at our tax policy, he would conclude it had been designed by a Communist spy to make free enterprise unworkable." But we cannot have such reform while our tax policy is engineered by people who view the tax as a means of achieving changes in our social structure. Senator Clark (D.-Pa.) says the tax issue is a class issue, and the government must use the tax to redistribute the wealth and earnings downward.

KARL MARX. On January 15th in the White House, the President told a group of citizens they were going to take all the money they thought was being unnecessarily spent, "take it from the have's and give it to the have-nots who need it so much." When Karl Marx said this he put it: . . . "from each according to his ability, to each according to his need."

Have we the courage and the will to face up to the immorality and discrimination of the progressive surtax, and demand a return to traditional proportionate taxation? Many decades ago the Scottish economist, John Ramsey McCulloch, said, "The moment you abandon the cardinal principle of exacting from all individuals the same proportion of their income or their property, you are at sea without a rudder or compass and there is no amount of injustice or folly you may not commit." No nation has survived the tax burden that reached one-third of its national income.

Today in our country the tax collector's share is 37 cents of every dollar earned. Freedom has never been so fragile, so close to slipping from our grasp. I wish I could give you some magic formula, but each of us must find his own role. One man in Virginia found what he could do, and dozens of business firms have followed his lead. Concerned because his 200 employees seemed unworried about government extravagance he conceived the idea of taking all of their withholding out of only the fourth paycheck each month. For three paydays his employees received their full salary. On the fourth payday all withholding was taken. He has one employee who owes him $4.70 each fourth payday. It only took one month to produce 200 conservatives.

Are you willing to spend time studying the issues, making yourself aware, and then conveying that information to family and friends? Will you resist the temptation to get a government handout for your community? Realize that the doctor's fight against socialized medicine is your fight. We can't socialize the doctors without socializing the patients. Recognize that government invasion of public power is eventually an assault upon your own business. . . . If some among you fear taking a stand because you are afraid of reprisals from customers, clients, or even government, recognize that you are just feeding the crocodile hoping he'll eat you last.

If all of this seems like a great deal of trouble think what's at stake. We are faced with the most evil enemy mankind has known in his long climb from the swamp to the stars. There can be no security anywhere in the free world if there is not fiscal and economic stability within the United States. Those who ask us to trade our freedom for the soup kitchen of the welfare state are architects of a policy of accommodation. They tell us that by avoiding a direct confrontation with the enemy he will learn to love us and give up his evil ways. All who oppose this idea are blanket indicted as war-mongers. Well let us set one thing straight, there is no argument with regard to peace and war. It is cheap demagoguery to suggest that anyone would want to send other people's sons to war. The only argument is with regard to the best way to avoid war. There is only one sure way—surrender.

APPEASEMENT OR COURAGE? The spectre our well-meaning liberal friends refuse to face is that their policy of accommodation is appeasement, and appeasement does not give you a choice between peace and war, only between fight or surrender. We are told that the problem is too complex for a simple answer. They are wrong. There is no easy answer, but there is a simple answer. We must have the courage to do what we know is morally right, and this policy of accommodation asks us to accept the greatest possible immorality. We are being asked to buy our safety from the threat of the Bomb by selling into permanent slavery our fellow human beings enslaved behind the Iron

Curtain, to tell them to give up their hope of freedom because we are ready to make a deal with their slave masters.

Alexander Hamilton warned us that a nation which can prefer disgrace to danger is prepared for a master and deserves one. Admittedly there is a risk in any course we follow. Choosing the high road cannot eliminate that risk. Already some of the architects of accommodation have hinted what their decision will be if their plan fails and we are faced with the final ultimatum. The English commentator Tynan has put it: he would rather live on his knees than die on his feet. Some of our own have said "Better Red than dead." If we are to believe that nothing is worth the dying, when did this begin? Should Moses have told the children of Israel to live in slavery rather than dare the wilderness? Should Christ have refused the Cross? Should the patriots at Concord Bridge have refused to fire the shot heard round the world? Are we to believe that all the martyrs of history died in vain?

You and I have a rendezvous with destiny. We can preserve for our children this the last best hope of man on earth or we can sentence them to take the first step into a thousand years of darkness. If we fail, at least let our children and our children's children say of us we justified our brief moment here. We did all that could be done.

INDEX

abortion laws, 201
Accidents Will Happen, 37
AFL-CIO, 76, 146, 159, 168
Air Force service, 45-50
Alexander, Jane, 91
American Medical Assn., 73
American Newspaper Guild, 57
Americans for Democratic Action, 52, 232
American Veterans Committee, 52, 55
Amish people, 243
Anderson, Glenn, 92, 144, 149, 173
Aptheker, Bettina, 122*n*
Aptheker, Herbert, 122*n*
Area Redevelopment Agency, 239
Army service, 44-45
Arnow, Max, 34
Auto Workers Union, 57

Bar Association, 126
Baroody, William, 77-79
Barrymore, Lionel, 41
Barry, Philip, 35
Battaglia, Phil, 141, 170, 177, 187, 203-205, 209
Baus and Ross, 146
Beck, Paul, 205
Beery, Wallace, 41
B films, 37
Berkeley demonstrations, 90, 122-123, 124, 140, 192
Betts, Bert A., 174
Birch Society. *See* John Birch Society
Birth of a Nation, The, 12
Bliss, Ray, 133
Bonanza, 73
Bond, Julian, 152
Booker, Phillip, 45
Boone, Pat, 158
Booz, Allen & Hamilton, 188
Bowron, Fletcher, 108
Bradley, Don, 144
Brennan, Walter, 158
Broder, David, 115, 132, 157
Brooke, Edward, 223

Brown, Pat, 89, 90, 91, 92*n*, 99, 105, 106, 108, 110, 112, 114, 115, 117, 118, 119, 122-123, 124, 129, 130, 131, 135, 136-137, 139, 140, 143-146, 149, 150, 151-170, 171-172, 174, 184*n*, 191, 194, 201, 203, 212, 221, 222, 232, 233
Brown, William L., Jr., 144
"Brunch with Barry," 78
Burns, Hugh, 143, 197
Burton, John, 220
Byrd, Harry, 241
Byrnes, John, 60

Calif. Citizens for Goldwater-Miller, 77, 88
Calif. Coordinating Council for Higher Education, 190*n*
Calif. Democratic Central Committee, 92, 97, 98, 144
Calif. Democratic Council, 119, 143, 153, 160
California Poll, 144, 152-153, 156, 161, 170, 216
Calif. Republican Assembly, 88, 91, 120, 121
Calif. Republican League, 99, 120
Calif. Senate Fact-Finding Committee on Un-American Activities, 53, 55, 121
Carmichael, Stokely, 168-169, 232
Carnegie Study of the Future of Higher Education, 193*n*
Castro, Fidel, 140, 235, 242
Chamberlain, John, 131
Champion, Hale, 198
Chandler, Dorothy, 192, 193
Chandler, George, 158
Chicago Cubs, 33, 35
Chicago *Tribune*, 132
Childs, Marquis, 124
Chinese Communists, 222, 232
Chow, David, 88
Choy, Wilbur W. Y., 7, 8
"Christian Anti-Communism Crusade," 148

Christopher, George, 74, 86, 92, 93, 97, 98, 99, 105, 106, 108, 113-117, 120, 121, 123, 129, 134, 135, 136, 145, 153
C.I.A., 153
Civil Rights Act, 116-117
Clarke, Thurmond, 38
Clark, Joseph S., 244
Clark, William P., Jr., 204, 205-206
Clausen, Don, 86
Clawson, Del, 86
Cleaver, Margaret, 16, 21
Coate, Robert L., 106, 143, 147, 148, 149
Coblentz, William, 155
Coke, Earl, 204, 207
Cole, Bud, 23
Connors, Chuck, 158
Copley News Service, 141, 205
Cordiner, Ralph, 70-71
Cornuelle, Richard, 210
Cowboy From Brooklyn, 37
Cranston, Alan, 146, 147, 174
Creative Society, The, 110, 125-128, 155, 172, 179, 184, 196, 200, 202, 207, 208, 210, 218, 227

Dalen, George, 69-70
Davies, Lawrence E., 113
Davis, Loyal, 61
Davis, Nancy, 61, 62, 75. *See also* Reagan, Nancy
Davis, Philip, 88
Death Valley Days, 75
Defense, Department of, 244
de Havilland, Olivia, 56
Dewey, Thomas E., 132
Diem regime, 222
Dirksen, Everett, 227
Dixon High School, 14-15
Dixon, Ill., 12-16, 27, 30
Donovan, Robert, 140
Douglas, Helen Gahagan, 74*n*
Drummond, Roscoe, 201, 216
Dunkel, Earl, 68-69
Dunne, Irene, 158
Duscha, Julius, 214
Dutton, Frederick, 144, 154

Ebsen, Buddy, 158
Eisenhower, Dwight D., 74*n*, 75, 94, 115, 132, 134, 137-139, 142, 174*n*, 223, 226, 227, 230

Eleventh Commandment, Parkinson's, 96, 97, 142
Estes, Billy Sol, 237
Eureka College, 16-17, 18-25, 28, 40
Evans, Rowland, 98, 157

Face the Nation, 169
Federal Housing Commission, 238
Federal Power Commission, 243
Federal Trade Commission, 243
Fellows, Robert, 39-40
Field, Mervin, 145, 161, 216
Field Poll. *See* California Poll
Finch, Robert H., 7, 134, 145, 166, 173, 184, 191, 209-211, 220
Firestone, Leonard, 134
Fleeson, Doris, 131
Flournoy, Houston L., 147, 174
Ford, Gerald, 226
Forsythe, John, 158
Fort Mason, 44, 45
Fort Roach, 46-50
Fortune magazine, 188, 196
Foy, Brynie, 39
Franklin, Benjamin (quoted), 8
Frawley, Patrick J., Jr., 148
Frazer, Bernard J., 15
Freedom Foundation Awards, 67
Freeman, Orville, 156
Free Speech Movement, 122*n*, 191
"Friends of Ronald Reagan," 88
Frizzelle, Nolan, 88
Futterman, Myron, 38

Gallup Poll, 219-220, 227, 229
General Electric Co., 65-71, 73, 168
Geneva agreement, 222
GE Theater, 65-67, 71, 73
Goldwater, Barry, 76, 77, 84, 85, 86, 92, 110*n*, 114, 130, 133, 136-137, 141, 146, 150, 156, 163, 223, 224, 226-227, 228, 232
Goldwater TV Committee, 78
Goodlett, Carlton B., 119
Grant, Allen, 191
Grant, Ulysses S., 14
Gray, William P., 120, 121
Great Society, The, 104, 125, 140, 155, 176*n*

INDEX

Greenburg, Carl, 107
Grizzly II, 195, 201
Gross, H. R., 31

Haffner, Fred, 87
Haldeman, Harry R., 191
Harris, Lou, 132
Hayden, Sterling, 54
Hearst, Mrs. Randolph, 193
Hellman, Marco, 142
HICCASP, 55-56
Higdon, Ernest E., 24
Hill, Gerald, 153
Ho Chi Minh, 232
Hodges, Joy, 34
Holden, William, 62
Hollywood Independent Citizens Committee (HICCASP), 55-56
Hoover, Herbert, 22
Hoover, J. Edgar, 94
House Committee on Education and Labor, 59
House Committee on Un-American Activities, 53, 54, 57, 58, 59, 77
Howell, Robert, 186
Hubber, Richard G., 21*n*
Human Events, 148
Humphrey, Hubert, 156, 159-160, 215

Independent Action, 210
Independent Sector, 210*n*
International Alliance of Theatrical Stage Employees, 53
International Commission of the Californias, 210

Jackson, Donald, 77
Jenkins, Walter, 232
John Birch Society, 74, 91, 92, 93-95, 100, 102-103, 139, 146, 147, 148, 149, 157, 163, 174
Johnson, Ellen Marie, 22
Johnson, Hiram, 85
Johnson, Lyndon, 91, 119, 140-141, 143, 169, 176*n*, 219, 220, 227, 228, 231, 232, 233
Johnson, Mrs. Lyndon, 156
Jordan, Frank M., 84, 174

Kearns, Doc, 32
Keating, Edward, 152
Kennedy, John F., 77, 140, 162-163, 231, 233

Kennedy, Robert, 154, 156, 165, 221, 222, 227
Kenya, 241
Kernoff, Judith, 205
Kerr, Clark, 121-123, 190-193, 201
Kershner, Howard, 241
Khrushchev, Nikita, 59, 140, 163, 232
Killers, The, 75
King's Row, 41-42, 44, 45
Kitchel, Denison, 77-78
Knight, Goodwin, 86, 88, 92, 98, 108, 113, 145, 191
Knott, Walter, 88, 148
Knowland, William, 86, 167*n*, 171
Knowles, Josiah P., 142
Knute Rockne, All American, 40
Krabach, Richard, 207
Krock, Arthur, 131
Kuchel, Thomas H., 74, 86, 88, 89, 92*n*, 98, 99, 114-115, 135, 136, 139, 141, 143, 145, 204, 225

Labor League of Hollywood Voters, 51
Laird, Mel, 226
Lancaster, Burt, 158
Lane, Thomas, 217
Laxalt, Paul, 225
Lebanon, 241
Le Roy, Mervyn, 61
Lewis, Ed "Strangler," 32
Lewis, Ted, 140
Life magazine, 60
Lipscomb, Glen, 142
Livermore, Norman, 204, 206-207
London *Observer,* 216
Long Beach State College, 190
Lopez, Trini, 158
Los Angeles Chamber of Commerce, 103, 126, 208
Los Angeles *Herald Examiner,* 132, 165-166, 167
Los Angeles Junior Chamber of Commerce, 141
Los Angeles magazine, 85
Los Angeles *Times,* 44, 107, 108, 130, 131, 140, 151, 153, 166-167, 205, 217
Lowell, James Russell, 16
Lowell Park, 15-16

250   REAGAN

Luce, Gordon, 204, 207
Luckett, Edith, 61
Lupino, Ida, 63
Lynch, Thomas C., 174, **177**

MacArthur, Peter, 27, 28
McBirnie, W. S., 11*n*
McCall, Tom, 224-225
McCann-Erickson agency, 33*n*
McCarthy, John F., 142
McCarthy, Joseph, 72, 192
McClellan, H. C. (Chad), 208
McComb, Marshall F., 7
McCone, John, 153, 154*n*
McCulloch, John Ramsey, 244
McDonald, Jack, 230
McHugh, Drake, 41
McHugh, Frank, 37
McKinzie, Ralph, 21, 22, 23
McNichol, R. A., 14-15
McPherson, Aimee Semple, 32

Madison, James (quoted), 235
"Man Against the Actor, A," 163-164
Management Council for Merit Employment Training & Research, 208
Marks, Milton, 220
Marx, Karl, 244
Mason, Lowell, 243
Mathias, Robert, 175
MCA, 60, 63, 64, 65, **142**
Medi-Cal, 197
Medicare, 73, 197
Meiklejohn, William, 34, 35
Mental Hygiene, Dept. of, 198-200
Meyer, Theodore R., 191, 192, 193
Milias, George W., 143
Mills Brothers, 32
Mills, Ed, 142
Monagan, Robert T., 98-99, **142**, 197
Moore, J. Max, 142
Morris, Wayne, 38
Moseley, C. C., 148
Motion Picture Industry Council, 58
Muchmore, Don, 172, 174, 213
Murphy, Franklin, 190
Murphy, George, 7, 8, 53-54, 77, 85, 106*n*, 134, 173, 187, 225, 230

National Federation of Republican Women, 230
National Labor Relations Board, 243
National Negro Republican Assembly, 116
National Press Club, 137, 140
NBC Radio (Chicago), 26-27
Nestor v. Fleming, 240
New Republic, 215
Newsweek, 124, 130, 132, 221, 222-223
N.Y. *Daily News*, 140, 157
N.Y. *Times*, 102, 113, 115, 116, 120, 124, 131, 132, 158, 161, 187, 192, 224
Nixon, Richard, 73-74, 77, 86, 88, 92, 141, 142, 145, 156, 162-163, 171, 172, 173, 204, 226, 227, 228, 229, 230, 231, 233
Nobbe, George, 157
Nofziger, Lyn, 141, 178, 203, 204, 205, 209
Northwestern University, 22, 23
Novak, Robert, 98, 157

Oakland riot, 160
Oakland *Tribune*, 167*n*
O'Brien, Pat, 37, 39
O'Donnell, Gladys, 230
Operation Austerity, 196, 198

Pacific Palisades, 75, 87, 134, 190
Palo Alto *Times*, 165
Parker, Fess, 158
Parker, William, 118
Parkinson, Gaylord, 96, 97, 136, 142
Patrick, William P., 99, 116, 117, 120
Pearson, Drew, 73, 135, 145
Peenemunde, Germany, 47
Penn, William (quoted), 155
Percy, Charles, 223, 229, 230
Pettis, Jerry, 175
Pike, Thomas A., 134
Plutarch (quoted), 236
Point Reyes Seashore, 156
Politician, The, 94
Post, Alan A., 111-112
Power and Politics, Conference on, 152
Pravda, 224

INDEX

Priest, Ivy Baker, 174
Proposition 1A, 211
Proposition 14, 123
Proposition 16, 115

Quinn, Richard (Sandy), 187, 204

Rafferty, Max, 162, 191
Ramparts magazine, 152, 161
Reader's Digest, 148
Reagan, Bruce, 88
Reagan, John Edward, 11-13, 27, 29-30, 38-39
Reagan, John Neil (Moon), 11-14, 22, 24, 26, 32-33, 42, 142
Reagan, Maureen Elizabeth, 38
Reagan, Michael, 38
Reagan, Nancy, 61, 62, 65, 84, 102, 212
Reagan, Nellie Clyde, 11-13, 79n
Reagan, Patricia Ann, 62, 212n
Reagan, Ronald Prescott, 62, 212n
Reclaiming the American Dream, 210
Redwood City *Tribune,* 166
Reed, Gordon, 231
Reimers, Ed, 31
Report to the People, 214-215
Republican Congressional Campaign Committee, 230
Republican Council of Calif., 120
Republican Governors' Assn., 230
Republican National Committee, 79, 141
Republican Senatorial Campaign Committee, 230
Republican State Central Committee, 92, 115
Reuther, Walter, 168
Revue Productions, 65
Reynolds, Nancy Clark, 205
Rhodes, James A., 207, 230
Ribicoff, Abraham, 154
Riesel, Victor, 159, 209
Ripon Society, 225
Riverside *Press Enterprise,* 166
Roberts, Bill, 87, 89, 91, 141, 170
Rockefeller, Nelson, 86, 92, 114, 141, 142, 150, 223, 224, 228, 229, 230
Rogers, Roy, 158

Romney, George, 223, 227, 229, 230
Roosevelt, Franklin D., 12, 22, 29, 51, 132
Rousselot, John, 74, 86, 91, 92, 100, 102, 148
Rubel, A. C. (Cy), 83, 87, 88, 134, 177
Rumford Act, 123, 144, 156, 165

Sacramento *Union,* 229
Salinger, Pierre, 77, 106
Salvatori, Henry, 83, 87, 88, 134, 148, 231
San Diego *Union,* 167n, 217
San Francisco *Chronicle,* 211, 222
San Francisco riot, 160
San Jose *News,* 167n
San Jose State College, 190
Santa Monica *Outlook,* 217
Saturday Evening Post, 124
Savio, Mario, 122n, 191
Schlei, Norbert S., 174
Schlicter, Sumner, 244
Schreiber, Taft, 60, 142
Schwarz, Fred, 148
Schuyler, George, 223-224
Scranton, William, 110n
Scratch, Walter, 217
Screen Actors Guild, 31, 38, 52-62
Senate Bill No. 268, 238
Shell, Joseph, 86, 88, 91, 92
Sherman, William T., 229n
Sills, Mrs. David, 38
Sinatra, Frank, 158
Smith, Al, 104, 132
Smith, Gordon, 188, 189, 208
Smith, Howard K., 133, 236
Smith, Robert M., 227
Social Security, 239-240, 243
Soviet Union, 133, 221, 241
Spencer-Roberts and Haffner, 86-87, 141
Spencer, Stu, 87, 89
"Stars of Tomorrow," 44
State College System, 210
State Department, 242
State Lands Commission, 210
State Poll, 108, 131, 156, 170
Stewart, James, 62, 89n
Student Non-Violent Coordinating Committee (SNCC), 152, 168

252 REAGAN

Supreme Court of California, 123

Taft, Robert, 230
Talmud, The, 105
"Target Is Your Family, The," 164
Taurog, Mrs. Norman, 88
Taylor, Robert, 34, 62, 75
Tennessee Valley Authority (TVA), 70, 237-238
Thant, U, 227
Thomas, Bob, 159
Thomas, Danny, 158, 187
"Time for Choosing, A," 77-80, 235-246
Time magazine, 79, 130
Tokyo in miniature, 47, 48
"Town Meeting of the World," 221
Truman, Harry, 51
Tuttle, Holmes P., 83, 87, 141
TVA, 70, 237-238
20th Century Fox, 75n

Udall, Stewart, 155
United Nations, 240, 242
United Republicans of California, 88, 120, 121
United States Manual, 241
United Student Aid Funds, 126
United World Federalists, 52
Universal Pictures, 63
University of California, 110, 121, 154, 156, 164, 168, 177, 188, 189-193, 198, 210
University of California at Los Angeles, 89, 110
University of Southern California, 125
Unruh, Jesse, 119, 143, 144, 160, 177, 191, 194, 197, 200
Urban Renewal, 238
U.S. News and World Report, 176
U.S.O., 45
U.S.S.R., 133, 221, 241
U Thant, 227

Valley State College, 190
Veterans Administration, 238
Vietnam war, 119, 122, 143, 164, 168, 186, 209, 222
Virginia Military Institute, 37

"Voice of Americanism," 110n
V-2 rocket sites, 47

Wagner, Lo Anne, 4
Wall Street Journal, 216
Warner Brothers Studios, 34, 40, 44, 56, 63
Warner, Jack, 35, 89
Warren, Charles, 144, 225
Warren, Earl, 145
Warschaw, Carmen, 144
Washington *Post,* 139, 157, 214
Waters, Laughlin, 92, 99-100, 107, 113
Watts community, 127, 208, 209
Watts riots, 90, 102, 118, 154n, 160, 173
Wayne, John, 158
Weaver, Warren, 158
Weinberger, Casper, 142
Weinrod, Bruce, 4
Welch, Robert, 94, 95, 139
Western State University, 28
WGN radio station, 26
Where's the Rest of Me? 21, 41-43, 93
White, F. Clifton, 227
White, William S., 131
WHO radio, 31
Wiggins, Charles, 175
Williams, Spencer, 174, 204, 206
Wilson, Bob, 230
Wilson, Burt, 18-19, 20
Wilson, Nancy, 158
Wilson, Richard, 140
WOC radio, 26, 27-28, 30-31, 33
Wood, Sam, 42
Works Progress Administration, 29, 30
Wright, Loyd, 74, 108, 148
Wyman, Eugene, 143
Wyman, Jane, 38

Yearling Row, 64, 75
You Can Trust the Communists (To Be Communists), 148
Young Americans for Freedom, 148
Young Republican National Federation convention, 224
Young Republicans, 230
Youth Aid Plans, 240-241
Yorty, Sam, 91, 118, 119, 129, 130, 136, 143, 152, 153, 154, 160, 161

A UNIQUE BOOK

RED primer for children and diplomats

by Victor Vashi

224 Pages of Satire and Clever Cartoons!

This is the chronological history of fifty years of Communism (1917-1967), the story of slaughter, butchery, murder, treachery, deceit, lies, broken promises and slave labor camps — all in powerful cartoons.

You will run the gamut of emotions, from side-splitting laughter to abject horror, terror and disgust.

This is a report of the oppression of proud and decent people by a handful of tyrants. It is authored by one of Hungary's top political cartoonists, Victor Vashi, who lived through the Soviet occupation of his native land.

Mail to: VIEWPOINT BOOKS
P.O. Box 9622, San Diego, California 92109

Quantity Prices: *"Red Primer for children and diplomats"*
1 copy $1; 3 copies $2; 10 copies $5; 25 copies $10;
100 copies $30; 500 copies $140; 1000 or more copies $.25 ea.

Please send me _____ copies. Payment of $ _____ enclosed.

Name _____

Address _____

City and State _____ Zip _____

On orders of 10 or more books, California residents add 5% sales tax. For Rush Orders Shipped Special Handling, add $1 per 100 bks. or fraction thereof.

Mail to VIEWPOINT BOOKS,
P.O. Box 9622, San Diego, Calif. 92109

Quantity Prices for ROAD TO REVOLUTION:
1 copy $1; 3 copies $2; 10 copies $5; 25 copies $10;
100 copies $30; 500 copies $125; 1000 copies or more $.20 each

Please send me_____copies. Payment of $_____enclosed.

Name_____

Address_____

City and State_____Zip_____

On orders of 10 or more books, Calif. residents add 5% sales tax. For rush orders shipped Special Handling, add $1 per 100 books or fraction thereof.

In June of 1964, just one month before the Harlem Riots shocked the American people into the realization that a racial civil war was possible in this country, Phillip Abbott Luce, the author of this book, met with four others in a secluded area of Central Park, New York City, to discuss the possibility of creating a guerrilla operation in the Negro ghettos. They were all Communists, members of the pro-Chinese Communist Progressive Labor Movement.

In 1965, Phillip Abbott Luce left the world of Communism. As a former member of a hard-core Communist organization, Mr. Luce's "behind the scenes" report in this, his latest book, has a vital and prophetic significance for all thinking Americans.

Road to Revolution:

Communist Guerrilla Warfare in the U.S.A.

A VITAL NEW BOOK BY PHILLIP ABBOTT LUCE

REAGAN

VIEWPOINT BOOKS
P.O. BOX 9622
SAN DIEGO, CALIF. 92109

Please send me _____ copies of the **"REAGAN" BOOK.**
Payment of $ _____ is enclosed (send check or money order).

NAME _____

ADDRESS _____

CITY _____ STATE _____ ZIP _____

On Orders for more than 3 books, California residents please add 5% sales tax.

Cut Out Or Tear Out And Mail

ORDER FORM

SEE OTHER SIDE FOR QUANTITY PRICES

FOR ADDITIONAL COPIES USE THIS CONVENIENT

Give

REAGAN
A Political Biography

to **all** *your friends.*

In quantities of 100 or more, this book costs no more than an average greeting card.

QUANTITY PRICES:

1 copy $1   10 copies: $5   100 copies: $30
3 copies: $2   25 copies: $10   500 copies: $140
1000 or more copies: $.25 ea.
(Convenient order form on back of this page)